Lernkrimi Englisch

TOD IM GRAND CANYON

Marlena Corcoran

Compact Verlag

Bisher sind in dieser Reihe erschienen:

- Compact Lernkrimi Englisch: Grundwortschatz, Aufbauwortschatz, Grammatik, Konversation
- Compact Lernkrimi Englisch GB/US: Grammatik, Konversation
- Compact Lernkrimi Business English: Wortschatz, Konversation
- Compact Lernkrimi Französisch: Grundwortschatz, Aufbauwortschatz, Grammatik, Konversation
- Compact Lernkrimi Italienisch: Grundwortschatz, Aufbauwortschatz, Grammatik, Konversation
- Compact Lernkrimi Spanisch: Grundwortschatz, Aufbauwortschatz, Grammatik, Konversation
- Compact Lernkrimi Deutsch: Grundwortschatz, Grammatik

In der Reihe Schüler-Lernkrimi sind erschienen:

- Compact Schüler-Lernkrimi Englisch
- Compact Schüler-Lernkrimi Französisch
- Compact Schüler-Lernkrimi Spanisch
- Compact Schüler-Lernkrimi Latein
- Compact Schüler-Lernkrimi Deutsch: Grammatik, Aufsatz
- Compact Schüler-Lernkrimi Mathematik

In der Reihe Lernthriller sind erschienen:

- Compact Lernthriller Englisch: Grundwortschatz, Aufbauwortschatz, Grammatik, Konversation

In der Reihe Lernstory Mystery sind erschienen:

- Compact Lernstory Mystery Englisch: Grundwortschatz, Aufbauwortschatz

Weitere Titel sind in Vorbereitung.

Chefredaktion: Dr. Angela Sendlinger
Redaktion: Grit Sperlich
Fachredaktion: Todd Michael Rives
Produktion: Wolfram Friedrich
Titelillustration: Karl Knospe
Typographischer Entwurf: Maria Seidel
Umschlaggestaltung: Carsten Abelbeck

ISBN-13: 978-3-8174-7572-8
ISBN-10: 3-8174-7572-1
7275724

Besuchen Sie uns im Internet: www.compactverlag.de

Vorwort

Mit dem neuen, spannenden Compact Lernkrimi können Sie Ihre Kenntnisse des britischen und des amerikanischen Englisch auf schnelle und einfache Weise vertiefen, auffrischen und überprüfen. Inspector Hudson erleichtert das Sprachtraining mit Action und Humor. Er und seine spannenden Kriminalfälle stehen im Mittelpunkt einer zusammenhängenden Story. Da Hudsons Fall sich dieses Mal in den USA abspielt, greift die Story den Unterschied zwischen britischem und amerikanischem Englisch auf.
Erläuterungen zur Kennzeichnung der sprachlichen Unterscheidungen finden Sie in den Benutzerhinweisen. Der Krimi wird auf jeder Seite durch abwechslungsreiche und kurzweilige Übungen ergänzt, die das Lernen unterhaltsam und spannend machen.
Prüfen Sie Ihr Englisch in Lückentexten, Zuordnungs- und Übersetzungsaufgaben, in Buchstabenspielen und Kreuzworträtseln und lernen Sie, britisches und amerikanisches Englisch zu unterscheiden! Ob im Bus oder in der Bahn, im Wartezimmer, zu Hause oder in der Mittagspause – das Sprachtraining im handlichen Format bietet die ideale Trainingsmöglichkeit für zwischendurch.
Schreiben Sie die Lösungen einfach ins Buch!
Die richtigen Antworten sind in einem eigenen Lösungsteil zusammengefasst.

Und nun kann die Spannung beginnen …

Viel Spaß und Erfolg!

Inhalt

Lernkrimi 6
Abschlusstest 123
Lösungen 133

Story

James Hudson arbeitet als Inspector bei der legendären Polizeibehörde Scotland Yard. Er ist einer der fähigsten Männer und wird immer dann zu Rate gezogen, wenn seine Kollegen mal wieder vor einem Rätsel stehen. Seine resolute und krimibegeisterte Haushälterin Miss Paddington unterstützt ihn stets mit liebevoller Fürsorge. Dieses Mal darf sie allerdings lediglich seine Koffer packen, denn Inspector Hudson macht eine Urlaubsreise in die USA.
Vor Ort nimmt Hudson an einer Tour durch den Grand Canyon Teil, die den verheißungsvollen Namen „Tod im Grand Canyon" trägt. Während der Tour erfährt Hudson nicht nur zahlreiche Anekdoten über die mysteriösen Todesfälle, die sich im Grand Canyon ereignet haben, sondern er gewinnt auch Einblicke in die Eigenheiten seiner unterschiedlichen amerikanischen Mitreisenden.
Doch aus dem spannenden Motto der Reise wird plötzlich bitterer Ernst. Als sich unerwartet ein tragisches Unglück ereignet und ein gewagtes Rettungsmanöver fehlschlägt, drängt sich die Frage auf: War es Mord oder Selbstmord? Kann Inspektor Hudson verhindern, dass die tödliche Anziehungskraft des Grand Canyon noch ein weiteres Menschenleben fordert?

Benutzerhinweise

Der Text ist grundsätzlich in britischem Englisch verfasst. Amerikanische Ausdrücke sind zusätzlich nach folgendem Prinzip kursiv gekennzeichnet: Gibt es amerikanische Entsprechungen für die verwendeten britischen Wörter, stehen diese bei der ersten Verwendung des Wortes nach den britischen Wörtern in Klammern kursiv. Bei der weiteren Verwendung der Wörter entfällt dieser Zusatz.
Für Dialoge und direkte Rede gilt: Spricht ein Brite, wird die oben erklärte Kennzeichnung verwendet. Handelt es sich um einen amerikanischen Sprecher, verwendet dieser die amerikanischen Ausdrücke, die kursiv gesetzt sind. Die britische Entsprechung eines amerikanischen Ausdrucks steht bei der erstmaligen Nennung des Wortes in Klammern hinter dem kursiven amerikanischen Wort. Ab der zweiten Nennung des Wortes steht nur noch der kursive amerikanische Ausdruck.
Steht nach einem britischen oder amerikanischen Ausdruck eine Übersetzung in Doppelklammern heißt dies, dass der so gekennzeichnete Ausdruck in beiden Sprachräumen verwendbar ist. Sagt ein Brite zum Beispiel *dear* im Sinne von „teuer", würde ein Amerikaner *expensive* sagen. *Expensive* kann man aber auch im britischen Englisch sagen – das Wort steht also kursiv in Doppelklammern hinter dem Wort *dear*.
Grundsätzlich wird bei der Einordnung von Wörtern als britisch bzw. amerikanisch die Auswahl nach der Häufigkeit der Verwendung des Wortes im jeweiligen Sprachraum bzw. nach der Herkunft des Wortes getroffen. Wird also zum Beispiel das Wort *sneakers* als amerikanischer Ausdruck gekennzeichnet, so heißt dies, dass das Wort im Amerikanischen häufiger verwendet wird bzw. dass es wie in diesem Fall ursprünglich aus dem Amerikanischen stammt und inzwischen manchmal auch im Britischen verwendet wird.

Tod im Grand Canyon

"Nearly six hundred people have lost their lives in Grand Canyon." Inspector James Hudson read this particular tour brochure with great interest. He had recently been to New York to help solve a case of armed robbery and murder committed by a leader of the Skyline Syndicate. His visit to New York had awakened his interest in the United States. When his supervisor, Sir Reginald, insisted that Hudson should take a holiday (*vacation*), Hudson's thoughts had turned to the vast western states.

"I'd like to see Grand Canyon," he thought. "And I might pick up a few tips on this tour." It was led by a guide who would tell them stories of murder, suicide and mishap at the various stages of the trail. "I'm not so sure about the white-water rafting," thought Hudson. "But perhaps I've grown a bit too cosy (*cozy*)."

! ÜBUNG 1

Übung 1: Unterstreichen Sie die acht Verben im Simple Past!

"Jolly good idea!" exclaimed Sir Reginald.

Hudson sat across from his supervisor at Scotland Yard, with the tour brochure in his hand.

"And never mind this nonsense about picking up tips!" continued Sir Reginald. "You are my finest detective, and you deserve a holiday! Here, let me have a look at that brochure."

Inspector Hudson handed the brochure to Sir Reginald.

"Well, sir, I'll fly from London to Chicago, and then on to Arizona. The state's name means 'arid zone', if my etymological knowledge from university serves me correctly."

"Will you lighten up, Hudson? Don't they have any girls at university these days?"

"Not at my college, sir."
"Why don't you take a few days in Chicago, as well? Frank Lloyd Wright and all that!"
Sir Reginald looked down at the tour brochure.
"My goodness!" gasped Sir Reginald. "Look at these cliffs! And those colours (*colors*)! It's nothing like England at all!"
"I'm afraid that's true, sir."
"I meant that in a positive sense, Hudson. Now please book this tour as soon as possible," ordered Sir Reginald. "I'm sure the change will do you good."

Inspector Hudson had a spring in his step as he opened the door to his tasteful flat (*apartment*), not far from Scotland Yard. He waved the tour brochure as he greeted his long-time housekeeper, Miss Paddington.

"My goodness, Mr (*Mr.*) Hudson!" exclaimed Miss Paddington. "You do seem cheerful today!"
"Kindly ((Please)) pack my bags, Miss Paddington! I am leaving on holiday tomorrow!"
"Such short notice, sir?"
"There was a free spot, Miss Paddington, and I'm off!"
His housekeeper looked at the brochure.
"'Death in Grand Canyon'? Mr Hudson, this seems a bit … wild, don't you think?"
"Not compared to the New York subway system," he replied. "Remember my recent adventures in New York?"
"Dead bodies everywhere in the dustbins (*garbage cans*), as I recall, sir," said Miss Paddington, with alarm.
"Oh, come now, Miss Paddington," laughed Hudson. "We've got them in Bath as well."

"I must admit, the view is incredible. And the colours! Why, this looks like no place on earth!"
Miss Paddington read more closely.
"And the list of clothing and equipment you must pack, sir! It's like an expedition to another planet!"
"It's America, not Mars," snapped Hudson, and whisked away the brochure. "Please don't bother about the hiking gear. I shall purchase all of that when I get off the plane in Arizona."

ÜBUNG 2 !

*Übung 2: Setzen Sie **a/an** oder **some** ein!*

1. ________ holiday 2. ________ brochure 3. ________ expedition
4. ________ case 5. ________ murder 6. ________ idea
7. ________ clothing 8. ________ education 9. ________ equipment

Many weary hours of travel later, Inspector Hudson woke up in a very large wooden travel lodge. It was hard to believe that this enormous hotel stood right at the rim of the Grand Canyon.
"Who had the idea to build a Victorian building here? It must have been the middle of nowhere at the time. How did it get here?" wondered Hudson.
Inspector Hudson yawned and stood up.
He almost fell right back down onto his bed.
"My goodness gracious!" he exclaimed. "I can't believe my eyes!"
The barest hint of moonlight picked out only the outlines of the gigantic natural wonder.
"Why, I might as well have awakened on Mars!" he gasped.
Hudson quickly looked back into the room to orient himself once again to a human scale of reality. His eyes fell on his alarm clock.

"Only three thirty!" he said to himself. "It's jet lag again!" Hudson remembered his experience with jet lag when he had visited New York.

Übung 3: Welches Wort ist das „schwarze Schaf"? Unterstreichen Sie das nicht in die Reihe passende Wort!

1. big, vast, huge, small, long
2. London, Chicago, Mars, England, New York, Arizona
3. holiday, tour, fly, supervisor, visit
4. murder, suicide, nonsense, accident, mishap
5. interest, cliff, canyon, desert, dry
6. college, school, Oxford, university, brochure

"At least jet lag is working in my favour (*favor*)," he thought. "I knew I'd have to be up well before dawn. The tour group must begin hiking early in order to avoid the heat of the day."

Hudson smiled when he saw the rucksack (*backpack*) he had carefully packed before he went to bed last night. He was not sorry he had decided to buy all his hiking equipment in Arizona. They knew just what he needed for a hike in Grand Canyon!

Inspector Hudson stepped into his pants (*underwear*), and then into loose, heavy cotton trousers (*pants*). He pulled on thick socks and laced up his well-worn hiking boots.

"They were well worth hauling over from England!" he thought. "Frightful ((Terrible)) scene at the airport, but I couldn't risk blisters from new boots!"

Hudson rummaged around in his luggage.

"This vest (*undershirt*) is not very stylish, I'm afraid!" he laughed, as he pulled on the first layer of quick-drying synthetic clothing.

"And Miss Paddington would faint if she saw the bright colour of this shirt! But I suppose it's just the ticket on the trail."
He tugged an equally colourful (*colorful*) pullover (*sweater*) over his head.

ÜBUNG 4 !

Übung 4: Geben Sie zu den folgenden Wörtern die amerikanische Schreibweise an!

1. colourful ____________________
2. honour ____________________
3. hour ____________________
4. savour ____________________
5. labour ____________________
6. flavour ____________________
7. our ____________________
8. favourite ____________________
9. glamourous ____________________
10. your ____________________

Feeling like a new man, Inspector Hudson went down to breakfast. The dining room of the grand old lodge was ringed with picture windows. The eerie moonlight hinted at the vast, unreal spaces that opened up just a hundred feet from the hotel.

"Good morning, sir," said a waitress, cheerfully. Clearly, she was accustomed to serving hearty breakfasts to hikers who wished to set out before dawn.

"Good morning," said Inspector Hudson.

"Oh!" she exclaimed. "You must be Inspector Hudson from Scotland Yard!"

"Is it that obvious?" asked Hudson. "I know I feel a bit out of place in my new clothing."

"It's easier to change your clothing than your accent," smiled the waitress. "We're very glad to see you. The rest of your group is seated by the window. They've all been waiting to meet you."

A suntanned man in the forest-green uniform of the National Park Service overheard the conversation. He walked towards (*toward*) Inspector Hudson and extended his hand.

"*Howdy* (How do you do?), Inspector Hudson! I'm Ranger Bob Snyder, the leader of the tour on 'Death in Grand Canyon'. I'm pleased to meet you."

"How do you do," said Inspector Hudson, warmly.

"You look surprised," said the ranger. "Are you having second thoughts about 'Death in Grand Canyon'?"

Inspector Hudson hesitated.

"Not at all. It's just that I have only heard people say 'howdy' in cowboy movies," admitted Inspector Hudson.

"Don't believe everything you see in the movies!" laughed Ranger Bob. "But you will hear 'howdy' a lot in the West. It's short for 'How do you do?'."

Übung 5: Was wird man wo in den verschiedenen Teilen der USA zu hören bekommen? Kreuzen Sie an!

ÜBUNG 5 !

1. Good morning!
   a) ☐ At breakfast anywhere in the United States.
   b) ☐ At dinner anywhere in the Unites States.

2. Howdy!
   a) ☐ When greeting someone in the West.
   b) ☐ When greeting someone in Boston.

3. Good afternoon!
   a) ☐ When parting in the evening.
   b) ☐ When ringing someone up in a big city.

4. Hello?
   a) ☐ When ringing someone up (*calling someone*) at home.
   b) ☐ When being introduced at a party.

5. So nice to see you!
   a) ☐ When meeting someone you know in the South.
   b) ☐ When saying goodbye at the New York airport.

6. Y'all come back!
   a) ☐ When arriving in Washington, DC.
   b) ☐ When leaving New Orleans.

Ranger Bob and Inspector Hudson sat down with four other people at the breakfast table.

"Good morning," they chorused.

"I'm Marie Johnson," said a pretty blond woman with an outdoorsy air. "And this is my husband, Paul."

"Paul Johnson," said a dependable-looking, dark-haired man with a pleasant smile, as he extended his hand.

"James Hudson," said the Inspector. "How do you do?"

"How do you do," said a thin, somewhat fragile-looking woman with light brown hair. "My name is Susan Gordon."

"And I'm Mel Gordon," said a man with broad shoulders and a muscular chest.

"James Hudson," repeated the Inspector. He had learnt (*learned*) in New York that Americans often call one another by their first names, whereas Britons would be more reserved.

Übung 6: Beantworten Sie die folgenden Fragen zum Text im Präsens!

1. What is Inspector Hudson's job?

____

2. In what city does he live?

____

3. What is Inspector Hudson's first name?

____

4. Is he American?

____

5. Does he usually wear colourful clothing?

____

6. Does Inspector Hudson own hiking boots?

____

7. Is Inspector Hudson hungry?

____

8. In what state is the Grand Canyon?

____

9. Does he feel out of place?

"We can recommend the scrambled eggs and sausage," volunteered Marie.
"If you're a vegetarian, the restaurant has other options," added the ranger. "But it's very important to pack in some protein before we get started."
"Sounds like the right moment for bangers and mash ((sausages and mashed potatoes))," observed Inspector Hudson.
His companions looked at him blankly.
"What you'd call sausages and mashed potatoes, I believe," smiled Inspector Hudson. "It's not something I'd normally eat under any circumstances, much less for breakfast. But we were all advised to eat a hearty breakfast! Let's see … Pancakes with maple syrup! I've never eaten that. *Oatmeal* (oatmeal porridge)? That must be oatmeal porridge."
Inspector Hudson hesitated.
"I think I'll have the eggs and rashers ((bacon))."
It was the waitresses' turn to look puzzled.
"Bacon and eggs," said the inspector, remembering the rather American idiom. "And a pot of tea, please."

ÜBUNG 7 !

Übung 7: Sind die folgenden Ausdrücke britisch, amerikanisch, oder beides?

1. oatmeal ____________
2. rashers ____________
3. eggs ____________

4. bacon ______________________

5. pancakes ______________________

6. tea ______________________

7. bangers and mash ______________________

8. cookie ______________________

9. breakfast ______________________

As Inspector Hudson was finishing his breakfast, Marie excused herself.

"I have to put on my hiking boots," she said. "I came to breakfast in *sneakers* (trainers)."

"It's time for all of you to gear up," said Ranger Bob.

"I have the checklist right here," said Mel. "I double-checked our *packs* (rucksacks) last night."

"I'll meet you in the *lobby* (reception) for inspection in fifteen minutes," said the ranger, amiably.

A quarter of an hour later, they listened to Ranger Bob tick off the items on the list.

"Moleskin, in case of blisters," he began. "A small signal mirror to flash for help in case of an emergency."

"I also brought a torch," volunteered Inspector Hudson.

"James, please! *Torches* are not allowed at all in the canyon," said Ranger Bob, sternly. "Open fire is too dangerous!"

"My mistake," said Inspector Hudson. "But it's a linguistic error. I believe you Americans call the item in question a *flashlight* (torch)."

Ranger Bob smiled. "Well, in that case, fine," he said. "It's the next item on the list."

Übung 8: Wie heißt das Simple Past der folgenden unregelmäßigen Verben?

1. begin ______________________
2. think ______________________
3. take ______________________
4. have ______________________
5. is ______________________
6. leave ______________________
7. buy ______________________
8. go ______________________

"Why do we have to carry all of this stuff?" asked Susan. "We'll only be gone for a few hours."

"One of the most important things you will learn on this tour," said Ranger Bob, "is how to avoid 'Death in Grand Canyon'! Many visitors to the canyon think we are running some sort of national amusement park here. I must warn you, however, that weather conditions in the canyon are extreme, and can change in a minute. Even on a day hike, we must be prepared for emergencies."

Mel looked at the ranger grimly.

"So," continued the ranger. "Does everybody have a whistle? Good. A first aid kit? A knife?"

Everyone nodded.

"We recommend several layers of light, quick-drying clothing," said the ranger, scanning the group quickly. "James, I'm not sure you're warm enough. The wind is up this morning."

"I'll get out my cagoule," agreed Inspector Hudson, and reached into his rucksack.
Once again, the Americans stared, wondering what magical item would appear from Inspector Hudson's rucksack.
"A *windbreaker* (windcheater)," said Marie.
"It's rainproof, too," confirmed Inspector Hudson.

Übung 9: Welche Wörter bezeichnen jeweils dasselbe Kleidungsstück? Ordnen Sie die britischen Wörter den amerikanischen Entsprechungen zu!

1. vest	☐	*sneakers*
2. trousers	☐	*windbreaker*
3. windcheater	☐	*underpants*
4. pullover	☐	*undershirt*
5. pants	☐	*pants*
6. trainers	☐	*sweater*

"The sun can be murder," said Ranger Bob. "I mean that literally. Has everyone got sunscreen, lip balm and sunglasses?"
"I brought tinted *moisturizer* (moisturiser)," announced Marie.
"You will now apply regular sunscreen," scolded the ranger.
"I brought an extra supply," said Mel, offering a tube to Marie.
"A hat," continued Bob.
"Yours is the best," admired Susan. "It's a genuine Smokey the Bear hat."
Ranger Bob smiled at Susan's allusion to the brown bear who symbolises ((symbolizes)) the National Park Service. The bear, like all rangers, wears the broad-brimmed hat that is the pride of the rangers of the National Park Service.

"Yes, *ma'am* (madam)," said Ranger Bob, tipping the brim of his hat with his fingers as a sign of politeness. "You can purchase one for yourself at our station, if you like."

Ranger Bob looked at Mel. "You checked out like a pro," he observed. "Have you had wilderness survival training?"

Susan looked nervously at her husband.

"No, sir," Mel said, shortly.

The ranger shrugged.

ÜBUNG 10

Übung 10: Stellen Sie zu den Antworten die richtigen Fragen! Achten Sie auf die Zeitform der Verben und verwenden Sie die Wörter ***what, where, how, whose, when, why, how much/many/often!***

1. This hat belongs to Ranger Bob.

___

2. He wears it every day.

___

3. It cost over a hundred dollars.

___

4. I don't know how he guessed the answer.

___

5. Inspector Hudson flew to Flagstaff, Arizona.

___

6. I don't know why Mel was so short with Bob.

___

7. The rangers recommended specific clothing.

8. Inspector Hudson arrived yesterday.

9. She had so many pullovers, she couldn't count them all.

10. You can purchase the hat at the station.

"I know you all had a hearty breakfast," he said. "And have you all brought suitable snacks for the trail? Nuts, raisins, *cookies* (biscuits), that sort of thing?"

Susan said that Mel had brought extra trail mix, just in case.

"I have *to go to the bathroom* (to use the toilet)," announced Marie.

"That reminds me," said the ranger. "We'll be stopping at rest stations today, but in principle, I want each of you to carry toilet paper with you, and a plastic bag. The toilet paper comes back out of the canyon in the bag to be disposed of back here. Our rule is: anything we take into the canyon, we take out of the canyon."

Marie ran to the ladies' toilet one last time.

"The last item is the most important one of all," stressed Ranger Bob. "Water. Simple dehydration has resulted in more deaths in Grand Canyon than any other cause. The National Park Service recommends that every hiker should carry at least one gallon of water for every day they plan to spend below the rim."

"A gallon of water weighs eight pounds," said Paul, skeptically.

! ÜBUNG 11

Übung 11: Setzen Sie die richtigen Zahlen ein!

1. There are ________ fluid ounces to a pint.
2. There are ________ pints to a quart.
3. There are ________ quarts to a gallon.
4. There are ________ inches to a foot.
5. There are ________ feet to a yard.
6. There are ________ inches to a yard.
7. There are ________ half-pints to a gallon.

"That should be your first clue," said Ranger Bob, "that a hike in Grand Canyon is not your ordinary stroll in the park. Water will be the heaviest item in any hiker's *pack*, and every hiker has to be able to carry it, or hike together with someone who can carry it for them."

"What if you can't?" asked Susan.

"We do have trails that are accessible to people with disabilities," explained Ranger Bob. "Such visits require careful planning, but we believe that Grand Canyon National Park has something to offer to visitors of all levels of ability. For the tour you have chosen, we stress that you must have a certain level of hiking ability, and above all, you must be able to carry the required amount of water."

Ranger Bob paused to admire Mel's rucksack. It was specially constructed to serve primarily as a water delivery system, but had pockets for clothing and gear.

"This system is excellent," pronounced the ranger, "because it focuses on the main thing: water."

"He got one for me, too," said Susan, glancing nervously at Mel. "And see, James has one, as well."

Inspector Hudson sensed Susan was trying to deflect attention from her husband.
"Let's get on with it," said Mel, gruffly.

Übung 12: Setzen Sie die folgenden Wörter in den Plural!

1. tour ____________________
2. robbery ____________________
3. murder ____________________
4. visit ____________________
5. holiday ____________________
6. state ____________________
7. person ____________________
8. life ____________________

The six hikers walked out into the surprisingly cold fresh air and headed off along the South Rim. At the entry to a trail that headed down into the canyon, they paused. The area was paved with stone, and a low stone wall ringed the area on the canyon side. On top of the wall was a guard rail. A sign read, 'Buena Vista'.
"This looks like a site designed to protect people from themselves," observed Mel.
"That's exactly right," agreed the ranger. "We understand that this spot will be many people's first full view of the canyon, away from any cars or buildings. The canyon drops off rather steeply here, so it's also many people's first experience of standing on the edge."

"I've heard it gets pretty crowded here in the summer," said Susan. "The pavement must help keep the ground from getting churned up by the boots of the thousands of hikers."

ÜBUNG 13 !

Übung 13: Bringen Sie den Dialog in die richtige Reihenfolge!

This is a good place from which to see Grand Canyon for the first time.

1. Don't they pay attention?
2. They climb over the guard rail.
3. Well, some of them do foolish things.
4. Unfortunately, all too many people fall off.
5. What do they do?
6. Do many people fall off?

Lösung: _ _ _ _ _ _

"It gets pretty crowded right here in the summer," agreed Bob. "But this early in the season, we shouldn't feel edged out."
"I'd hate to feel pushed around," Susan said. "It's so peaceful here right now."
"And if people do experience a bit of vertigo," said Bob, "they can orient themselves by looking at the stone paving, which is made by human hands; or by looking at the trees, which are on a more human scale."
Every member of the group looked instinctively for the trees.
"The stone wall and the guard rail must help, too," said Mel.
"They frame the view," agreed Bob. "And of course, they help keep people from falling over the edge!"
Marie was the only one who laughed.

Übung 14: Übersetzen Sie und enträtseln Sie das Lösungswort!

1. Pflaster _ _ □ _ _ _ _ _
2. gestaltet _ □ _ _ _ _ _ _
3. Mord _ _ □ _ _ _
4. Hut _ _ □
5. Pfad _ _ _ □ _
6. Parkwächter _ _ _ □ _ _
7. Kleidung _ _ □ _ _ _ _ _

Lösung: _ _ _ _ _ _ _

"I see you've got your camera out already, Paul," said the ranger. "This is a *favorite* (favourite) spot from which to take pictures. You might want to save your film – or your memory card – until it gets a bit brighter, though. And you might want to pay attention first while I tell you about some of the photographers who took – or posed for – their last picture on this very spot.
You'd think you were safe up here. I mean, how much more could we do?" asked Bob, gesturing at the stone wall and the guard rail. "But the rim is one of the most lethal locations in Grand Canyon. Fifty people have died of accidental falls from the rim – and twenty per cent (*percent*) of those people were either posing for or taking photographs."

Übung 15: Setzen Sie die Verben ins Simple Past!

"Let me tell you the story of Gregory Smynoff," (1. begin) ________________ Ranger Bob. "He and his girlfriend were walking back to the hotel along this very road late one evening, when he (2. jump) ______________________ up on the stone wall there and (3. start) ______________________ clowning around.

'Take my picture!' he cried. 'Take it quickly, before I fall!'

'Get off of there, Greg,' his girlfriend (4. scold) ______________.

'Don't be a *jerk* ((idiot)).'

Mr. (Mr) Smynoff (5. pretend) ______________________ to lose his balance, according to his girlfriend. She (6. turn) ______________________ her back on him and (7. continue) ______________________ back to the hotel, thinking that without an audience, he would stop the nonsense and follow her back to join the rest of their friends.

Mr. Smynoff never arrived.

His girlfriend, alarmed, (8. notify) ______________________ the *desk clerk* (receptionist) at the hotel. Two rangers (9. run) ______________________ back along the path you have just taken to this overlook.

The members of the search party peered over that low stone wall. There's a narrow ledge, just about a yard wide, not six feet below the wall. If a person dropped straight down, they just might be able to follow the ledge upwards to where it gets within an arm's length of the stone wall again, about twenty feet to our left.
But there was no trace of *Mr.* Smynoff.

Mr. Smynoff's girlfriend was convinced that he had climbed back up and was hiding somewhere in the bushes, too embarrassed to show his face."

Übung 16: Welche Gegenteile gehören zusammen? Setzen Sie die passende Ziffer ein!

1. embarrassed	☐ beginning
2. polite	☐ dusk
3. early	☐ proud
4. finishing	☐ unfashionable
5. magical	☐ playing
6. dawn	☐ late
7. stylish	☐ rational
8. working	☐ rude

"A rescue helicopter lifted off and searched for *Mr.* Smynoff, using infrared sensors. About six hundred feet below the rim here, they identified something that barely registered on their detection devices: *Mr.* Smynoff's body had already cooled to the point that they knew he was dead.
The rangers' best guess was that he missed his footing on that ledge just below, and bounced off into the wild blue yonder."

The Johnsons and the Gordons huddled together in the pre-dawn chill.
"That's horrible," said Susan.
"It is," said the ranger. "No disrespect to the dead intended, but I should probably mention that ..." The ranger sighed. "The role of alcohol is not to be excluded."

Übung 17: Verwandeln Sie die folgenden Adjektive in Adverbien!

1. regular ____________________
2. genuine ____________________
3. hearty ____________________
4. clear ____________________
5. short ____________________
6. pleasant ____________________
7. broad ____________________

"Do a lot of people fall?" asked Marie.
"If they didn't, there wouldn't be much material for this tour," snapped Mel.
Susan stiffened.
"Oh, I'm sorry, Marie," sighed Mel. "It's just that –."
"It happens," said Marie. "I understand."
"I've always wondered why people want to hear about this sort of thing just as they are about to brave Grand Canyon themselves," said Bob. "But it seems they can't get enough of these stories. 'Death in Grand Canyon' is one of our most popular tours."
"Tell me another," said Marie. "I love scary stories."

Übung 18: Ordnen Sie die Buchstaben zu einem sinnvollen Verb!

"I'd have a lot to (1. osoehc) ____________ from, unfortunately," replied Bob. "How about Melissa Gilhooley? She (2. tspepde) ____________ up onto that stone wall to (3. etg) ____________ a better view of the canyon."

Mel (4. popddre) ____________ his head into his hands. "Better than what?" he (5. ergodan) ____________.

"It (6. ssmee) ____________ she (7. nwdate) ____________ to (8. kloo) ____________ down and see just how steep that drop might be," said Bob. "Just then her boyfriend (9. cdalel) ____________ to her to (10. rtnu) ____________ around so he could (11. keat) ____________ her picture. She (12. tdfeli) ____________ her arms to pose – and over she (13. twne) ____________."

"I don't suppose that ledge did her any good," remarked Paul.
"No chance," said Bob. "There weren't even scuff marks on the rock."
Marie tucked her boots tighter under her.
"But I do know of a case where being on the ledge was itself the problem," continued Bob. "There was a homeless person drifting around here in the 1960s. He called himself 'Spider'. He used to jump around on the rocks, encouraging tourists to take his picture. They often gave him money.
One summer day he was working the crowd right here. Every one of the twenty-five people in the crowd said afterwards that he dared the tourists to throw him coins, which he promised to catch.
He did it, too. He was a sure-footed old goat, and had a lot of *practice* (practise) out there on the rocks.
Well, somebody threw him a dollar."
"Oh, no," moaned Mel.

"And it caught on the breeze." Ranger Bob nodded. "Just like a little parachute. Old Spider made a lunge for it, and –."
Mel stood up. "Excuse me," he said, and headed for the toilets.
Marie looked upset. "Maybe that's enough for now," she suggested.
"Fine," said Ranger Bob. "It's about time we headed down into the canyon."

ÜBUNG 19 !

Übung 19: Ordnen Sie die Übersetzungen richtig zu!

1. flat	☐ aufwachen
2. adventure	☐ unglaublich
3. raft	☐ Körper
4. awaken	☐ sich stürzen
5. incredible	☐ Fallschirm
6. body	☐ Abenteuer
7. ledge	☐ Floß
8. parachute	☐ sich wagen
9. lunge	☐ Felsvorsprung
10. dare	☐ Wohnung

The little group started its descent into the canyon. They hiked steadily on, as the sky brightened. Within the hour, they were standing on an open stretch of trail, gaping at the magnificent display of colour as the sun came up over Grand Canyon.
"I knew you'd want to get a first look at Grand Canyon at *sunup* (sunrise)," said Ranger Bob. He smiled at the expressions on the faces of the five hikers. Marie's jaw was literally hanging open.
"I've never seen anything so beautiful," said Susan, fervently. "Nothing prepares you for this." She stretched out her hand towards the vast spaces that opened out before them. "It's not human."

Übung 20: Unterstreichen Sie jeweils die richtige Präposition!

ÜBUNG 20 !

"Most 1. from/of the spaces we humans live in are 2. in/on a very different scale," agreed the ranger.
"I've never seen a part 3. from/of the earth that looked so … indifferent 4. to/from us," Susan said. "It doesn't matter, does it, whether we're here or not?"
The group stared and stared, as if waiting 5. for/on the moment when the canyon would suddenly reshape itself 6. into/in something more welcoming.
"It just goes on and on," said Susan. "Miles and miles 7. for/of a world that will never be ours."

"I have never thought I was a fan of *suburbia* ((the suburbs))," admitted Paul. "But suddenly I see the suburbs as awfully friendly. I guess we're used to projecting human life everywhere. It doesn't work here, does it? It's like Susan says. Looking at this, it's hard to imagine Grand Canyon covered with rows of houses."
"The National Parks are dedicated to the preservation of wilderness," said Ranger Bob. "There are other parks that are more threatened by human expansion. They have resources, such as minerals, that people are always looking at jealously."
Ranger Bob sighed.

*Übung 21: In welchem Satz ist **to** nicht Teil eines Verbs? Unterstreichen Sie!*

ÜBUNG 21 !

"The situation is more complicated in the National Forests," he explained. "In fact, the National Forests were originally called 'forest reserves', 1. **to** make clear that no logging was 2. **to** take place on those lands. That was in the late 1800s, when there was a great demand for timber in the United States, and logging was getting out of control. Even today, though, it's hard for people 3. **to** look at forests and not 4. **to** calculate how much money could be made by cutting down those trees. And I'm afraid that the National Forests now do sometimes offer forests for sale 5. **to** timber companies."

"Not many trees in the canyon," remarked Mel. "Looks pretty desolate down there."
"In a sense, we're lucky here," said Ranger Bob. "Grand Canyon is more intimidating than many other areas that were set aside as National Parks."
Susan gazed out over the canyon.

ÜBUNG 22 !

Übung 22: Unterstreichen Sie im folgenden Abschnitt die sechs Possessivpronomen!

"I think I'd like some *candy* ((sweets))," said Marie, rummaging in her rucksack. "Here, Paul. Would you like one?"
Mel frowned. "Remember to put the wrapper back in your *pack*, Marie."
Paul put his wrapper in his rucksack immediately.
"In fact, this is as good a place as any to take our rest break," said Ranger Bob. "We'll take ten minutes every hour to eat something, drink, and put our feet up."

Susan sighed. "Things like that seem so trivial out here," she said. "I mean, really – *candy*?" Ranger Bob looked concerned.
"We have to be careful, Susan," the ranger warned. "It's easy to get disoriented while looking at the canyon. It's a grand sight, to be

sure. But we need to remember the basic things like food, water and rest. Otherwise, we endanger our lives."
"I can't help but think," said Susan, "that our lives are rather small, compared to this."
Mel took Susan's hand and led her back into the shade of a ponderosa pine.
"Come on, honey," he said. "That's no way to think."

*Übung 23: Setzen Sie die richtige Form von **get** (im Sinne von **become**) ein! Achten Sie auf die Zeitform!*

ÜBUNG 23 !

1. It's easy ________________ disoriented in Grand Canyon.

2. Things can ________________ out of control.

3. The trail ________________ dusty in the summer.

4. Grand Canyon National Park ________________ crowded in July.

5. The sky ________________ brighter every day at dawn.

6. We ________________ thirsty before we had hiked for an hour.

7. Do you ________________ hungry by noon?

8. They ________________ horribly sunburned.

"We may not have many trees in Grand Canyon, with the exception of the forests on the North Rim," said Bob, "but the history of the Grand Canyon, at least as far as white people are concerned, is tied to the desire to strike it rich."
"Were they looking for gold?" asked Paul.
"Seven cities of gold," nodded Ranger Bob. "The Spanish explorer

Francisco Vásquez de Coronado believed there were seven cities of gold somewhere around here. Coronado sent Garcia Lopez de Cardenas with a small scouting party to look for the treasure here in the northern part of the territory known as New Spain."

"Did he find it?"

Ranger Bob snorted. "I'm afraid not. They did get about a third of the way down to the river, but by that point, it was clear that this was not a good idea."

"It must have been hard for Cardenas to explain what he did find," mused Susan. "Who would have believed him?"

"Another two hundred years went by before the next Spanish explorer, Francisco Tomás Garcés, arrived. Garcés stayed with the Havasupai Indians. The Havasupai had set up an irrigation system that Garcés admired. It was Garcés who gave a Spanish name to the river that cuts through the canyon. He called it the 'Colorado'."

ÜBUNG 24 !

Übung 24: Unterstreichen Sie im folgenden Abschnitt alle Wörter, die sich auf Farben beziehen!

"It certainly is *colorful* (colourful) around here," agreed Mel. "It's like another planet." They all found it hard to take their eyes off the play of crimson, orange and yellow on the towering cliffs, as day worked its way into Grand Canyon.

"The heyday of prospecting," continued Ranger Bob, "was the nineteenth century. Hundreds of claims were staked in Grand Canyon."

"Gold again?" asked Paul.

"Gold was discovered in California in 1849," said Bob. "There was none here, but later in the century, people were looking for copper, asbestos, silver and lead."

"Maybe it sounded like a good idea," speculated Mel, "if you'd never laid eyes on this place."
They looked out again over the bleak landscape. Deep violet and dusty blue in the depths of the canyon were giving way to the azure and turquoise of mid-morning.

"Pretty discouraging," agreed Bob. "But Grand Canyon benefited indirectly from the California Gold Rush. In order to get to California, people needed maps. The United States government funded extensive surveys to map the entire Southwest, which we had recently acquired at the close of the war with Mexico."
"That's an awful lot of land to survey," remarked Mel.
"It certainly was," agreed Bob. "Together with the Louisiana Purchase of 1803, the land acquired from Mexico in 1848 just about doubled the former size of the United States. The government in Washington hardly knew where it all was!
Mapping out such a vast territory was a huge undertaking. Sometimes private people got into the act. That brings us to John Wesley Powell, and the first murder story."
Ranger Bob looked down at his watch and up at the sky. "But you know what? It's time we got on our way. It takes twice as long to climb back out of the canyon, and I'd like to complete our descent before the sun gets too much higher."

Übung 25: Setzen Sie die Sätze ins Passiv!

1. The United States acquired western territory.

____

2. Surveyors mapped the land.

3. France sold Louisiana.

4. The sun lit up the canyon.

5. Ranger Bob told the story.

6. Francisco Tomás Garcés named the Colorado River.

7. Powell explored the Colorado River.

The little group continued its steep descent into the canyon. The terrain changed, and soon they were stepping from rock to rock.

"You were right, Bob," mumbled Paul. "This last part is pretty tough."

"People often don't realize (realise) how rough the hike can get," said the ranger. They read the distances on a map, and think, 'Half a mile? That's nothing!'."

"Could we stop for a minute?" asked Marie. "I need to get out my water bottle."

"The real trick," advised the ranger, "is to drink before you're thirsty. So drink up, everybody!"

They hiked in silence, carefully stepping from rock to rock. The trail evened out at last, and followed a jagged cliff that rose five hundred feet straight up above them. They marched along in single file. Up ahead, the cliff suddenly stopped, and the trail seemed to reach a dead end.

"I'm not going there," announced Susan. "I'm afraid."
"It's alright," said the ranger. "The cliff projects out right here, but the trail follows the turn in the cliff. We're just turning a corner."
Susan looked ahead. It seemed there was nothing but blue sky and Grand Canyon. She shook her head.
"No!"

Übung 26: Geben Sie die verneinte Form an! Verwenden Sie je nach Vorgabe die Kurzform!

1. You are afraid.

2. You are afraid. (Kurzform)

3. They are thirsty.

4. They are thirsty. (Kurzform)

5. You were right.

6. You were right. (Kurzform)

---

7. She is going.

---

8. She is going. (Kurzform)

---

9. I am going.

---

10. I am going. (Kurzform)

"I'll go ahead and check it out," said Mel, softly. "I'll go first, Susan."
"We'll stay here and eat a bit," suggested the ranger.

Mel was back in a few minutes.
"The ranger was right, Susan," he said. "The trail hugs the cliff, and turns to the right. It's just as wide as it is here, and there's a guard rail along the trail as it curves around."
"Alright," said Susan. "Alright. I feel better now, after I ate a bit."
"It isn't far to the rest area," Bob assured them. "That area is wider and more protected. There are trees under which we can rest up and gather our strength."
It wasn't long before the hikers were stretched out under pine trees at the rest area.
"I didn't think I'd really be up to a picnic lunch at eight o'clock in the morning," smiled Paul, "but I'm starved!"

Übung 27: Übersetzen Sie die folgenden Wörter, die im Englischen alle auf ***-ght*** *enden!*

1. Nacht ______________________
2. Licht ______________________
3. Macht ______________________
4. Flug ______________________
5. acht ______________________
6. Fracht ______________________
7. Flucht ______________________
8. gedacht ______________________

"You must be even hungrier than we are, James," observed Mel. "After all, it's dinner time in England."

"I'm famished," admitted Inspector Hudson, as he unpacked a sandwich that the hotel staff had prepared for him. "But I wouldn't have missed this for the world. That was quite some view down to the Colorado River."

"I thought it would be better if I didn't even mention that it was coming up," smiled Bob. "Nobody has to look down if they don't want to."

"I had read about that view," said Mel. "I saw a picture, too. It's over three thousand feet down to the Colorado."

"You really did your homework," said Bob. "Susan, you look a bit pale."

"I had seen that photo, too," she said. "But it's nothing like looking down at the river in real life."

"I'm not even sure it was worth bringing my camera," agreed Paul. "And from what Ranger Bob tells us, taking pictures can be fatal!" The other hikers laughed.

"A photograph is just –." Susan waved her hand as if brushing away a fly. "Out here, you're surrounded by the experience. It's 360 degrees of …"

"Of something very hard to express," agreed Inspector Hudson. "It's just so … big!"

They all laughed again.

"I feel a little lost," admitted Susan.

ÜBUNG 28 !

Übung 28: Lesen Sie Ranger Bobs Geschichte und entscheiden Sie: Welches Wort gehört in die Lücke?
(disaster, dwindling, settled, ferocious, quit, unable, explore, Powell, smashed, equipment, underway)

"Well, that brings us back to John Wesley 1. ________________," began Ranger Bob. The hikers all 2. ________________ in for a story. "He and his crew set out to 3. ________________ and map the Colorado River."

"I've heard of John Wesley Powell," said Paul. "Wasn't that trip a 4. ________________?"

"From beginning to end," sighed Ranger Bob. "It's hard to imagine how 5. ________________ the rapids can be. The four boats were solidly built oak boats, but they took on tons of water when running the rapids. They had only been 6. _______________ a couple of weeks when one of the boats 7. _______________ to pieces on the rocks, taking fully one third of their food and 8. _______________ with it. They still had nine and a half months to go."

Marie looked at her own 9. _______________ supply of food and water and sighed.

"One of the crew members 10. _______________ after that," continued Bob. "Powell himself was 11. _______________ to row, as he had lost an arm in the War between the States.

The men were soon on starvation rations. Powell had no talent for leadership, to put it mildly. On top of the physical hardship of the journey, there were serious morale problems.

This soon peaked in a fight between Powell and a mountain man on the crew, William Dunn. Powell assigned Dunn to a very dangerous post, from which he was knocked into the Colorado and almost drowned. It so happened that Dunn was carrying Powell's pocket watch, which was ruined in the water.

Powell shouted that Dunn could drown, for all he cared, but that the watch was a real loss. Powell insisted that Dunn should pay him for the watch on the spot or leave. There was, of course, no way out of the canyon at that point.

Not much farther downstream, Powell tried to drown Dunn. In short, this set off a fistfight in which members of the crew threatened to kill one another – and tried it, too."

"Sounds great," said Mel, sarcastically. "Excellent commanding officer. Real camaraderie."

ÜBUNG 29 !

Übung 29: Vervollständigen Sie die Sätze mit ***everywhere, anything, nothing, everybody, nobody, anywhere, anybody!***

1. ________________ on Powell's expedition was happy.

2. They had almost ________________ to eat.

3. ________________ could see it was too dangerous.

4. ________________ would make Powell see reason.

5. It might have happened ________________.

6. ________________ agreed that he was not a good leader.

7. ________________ they looked, they saw danger.

8. The crew would give ________________ to get out of there.

"The crew threatened to mutiny," confirmed Bob. "In fact, Dunn and two others, the Howland brothers, decided to get out of the canyon on foot, at the spot that is now known as Separation Rapid. This is a bad stretch of white water, and the three had decided that they no longer trusted Powell's *judgment* (judgement).

The six men in the boats got safely through the rapids, and fired their guns to let the three others know they could hike over and join the boats again. They claimed later that they waited until it was clear that the three others would not come back."

ÜBUNG 30 !

Übung 30: Wie sicher sind sich die Sprecher? Ordnen Sie zu und schreiben Sie die entsprechende Ziffer in das Kästchen!

1. He claimed	☐ that it didn't seem likely.
2. She insisted	☐ to say what might have happened.

3. He confirmed ☐ the truth of the story.
4. She objected ☐ he knew nothing about it.
5. He guessed, ☐ on doing it her way.
6. They hesitated ☐ but he wasn't sure.

"It's only seventy miles from Separation Rapid to Rio Virgin, Powell's end point. He told the Mormons there that three of his crew were hiking out of the canyon, and might need help.
Powell also said something rather foolish. He told the Mormons that the three hikers were carrying a chronometer worth six hundred and fifty dollars, and a valuable watch that had been given to them by Sumner, one of the men who had stayed with the boats. Sumner wanted them to give the watch to his sister in the event that he did not make it home alive.
Eight days later, a newspaper carried a story that Dunn and the Howlands had been murdered. The story said that the three men had killed an Indian woman, and that they had been killed by Indians in retaliation."

Übung 31: Setzen Sie die folgenden Sätze in die indirekte Rede!

ÜBUNG 31 !

1. "They murdered an Indian woman," he claimed.

____

2. "I gave them my watch for safekeeping," testified Sumner.

____

____

3. "The watch was very valuable," his sister confirmed.

____

4. “He was a terrible leader,” grumbled his men.

5. “Powell tried to kill me,” said Dunn.

6. “We no longer trust Powell,” said the men, after the attack on Dunn.

7. “Why should I believe you?” Powell asked Sumner.

8. “We still believe that Powell was a hero,” say many Westerners.

“There are several versions of that story, which in itself seems a bit suspicious. The stories are also not exactly plausible, for reasons having to do with the Indian wars and the way things stood with the Mormons at the time. Nonetheless, everybody left it at that, except for one man. Sumner reported that one day, he saw his watch – in the possession of a white man.”

Inspector Hudson sighed. “So in all likelihood,” he said, “Dunn and the Howland brothers were murdered by white men who were after their possessions.”

“The Native Americans were not exactly well treated, were they?” said Paul, his mouth tight.

"No, they were not," said Bob. "You will learn more about them in a couple of days. I understand you'll be driving over to Havasu Canyon and hiking down to the Supai Village."
"We'll hike to the falls and go swimming!" exclaimed Marie.
"Which sounds really attractive after three days of desert heat," added Paul.

Übung 32: Welches Relativpronomen ist korrekt?
(that, which, who, whom, whose)

1. The girl ______________ lost her cat put up a sign.

2. The man ______________ car was stolen reported it to the police.

3. That's the man ________________ I dislike.

4. The colour ________________ I like most is blue.

5. What's the name of the artist ______________ won the prize?

6. He could not take a stand on the two issues ______________ are of greatest importance to us.

7. That's the notebook ______________ I lost yesterday!

8. The students _________________ were admitted are very happy.

"For now," continued Bob, "I'll just mention that there is evidence that people passed through this canyon over ten thousand years ago. Between 7000 and 1000 BCE, there were archaic cultures in the canyon. Evidence of Puebloan culture has been dated to the era between 1000 BCE and 1300 CE. These people made baskets and

pottery, and you've probably seen pictures of their cliff dwellings."
"What happened to them?" asked Inspector Hudson.
"It's still somewhat of a mystery," replied Bob. "Though there is evidence of a great drought around 1150. It may have left the farming communities more vulnerable to invasion.
As the Pueblo Indians left, others came to settle here. They were the ancestors of today's Havasupai and Hualapai. Paiute Indians came up from the south and settled here as well. They were not farmers, but a hunter-gatherer tribe."
"Didn't you say that the man who gave the Colorado River its Spanish name stayed with the Havasupai?" asked Inspector Hudson.
"That's right," said Bob. "And you'll be staying with them three nights from now."

ÜBUNG 33 !

Übung 33: Welche Sätze stehen in der richtigen Vergangenheitsformen? Markieren Sie mit richtig ✔ oder falsch –!

1. The first human beings passed through the canyon in the Stone Age. ☐
2. The first people have not stay. ☐
3. The Pueblo Indians had living in cliff dwellings. ☐
4. The Pueblo Indians left as the Havasupai and Hualapai were coming. ☐
5. People were farmed in the canyon. ☐
6. A Spanish explorer stayed with the Havasupai. ☐
7. The Pueblo Indians may have left around 1150 because there was a drought. ☐
8. Paiute Indians come up from the South and had settled here. ☐

9. There were people living in Grand Canyon when the first white men came. ☐
10. The Indians who live in Grand Canyon today arrived about 400 years before the first European explorer came. ☐

"What about the Navajo Indians?" asked Mel. "Don't they live around here?"
"They sure do (They do, indeed)," said Bob. "And I'm afraid their story belongs to any account of death around, if not in, Grand Canyon."
"The Navajo death march?" asked Inspector Hudson.
"There were several episodes to the disgraceful event the Navajo call 'The Long Walk'," said Bob. "In 1864-65, after their defeat by the U.S. Cavalry, thousands of Navajo Indians were forced to walk to Fort Sumner, in New Mexico. Anyone who was tired or sick, or any pregnant woman who went into *labor* (labour), was shot. Anyone who stopped to help someone else was shot."
A long silence reigned.
"The Navajo live to the east of Grand Canyon now," said Bob. "They sometimes come here and sell rugs. You may meet some of them before you leave."
The group sat for awhile, lost in thought.
"We should gather our things and be on our way, before we stiffen up," suggested Bob.

ÜBUNG 34 !

Übung 34: Wer waren die indianischen Ureinwohner? Setzen Sie die Namen der Stämme ein!

1. ______________________ Indians came up from the South to Grand Canyon.

2. Many ________________ Indians died on the forced march to New Mexico.

3. The ________________ used irrigation to grow food in Grand Canyon.

4. ________________ Indians lived in cliff dwellings, and made baskets and pottery.

5. Kachina dolls are made by the ________________ tribe.

6. A great waterfall is found on the lands of the ________________, near Grand Canyon.

Just as they had been warned, the way up took twice as long as the way down. The sun was higher in the sky now, and temperatures on the exposed rock climbed into the eighties. Inspector Hudson was glad he had purchased several layers of clothing, which he peeled off one by one.

"That's enough of the old cagoule, eh?" teased Paul.

Inspector Hudson was too tired to laugh.

"We'll rest frequently on the way up," Bob assured them.

They found seats on a rock formation, and raised their feet. They found they were too tired to be picky about the location. Marie flopped down and got out her water bottle.

"I thought it was ridiculous to carry all this water," she said. "I couldn't imagine that I would be able to drink it all."

"This is where Bob's hat comes in handy, too," remarked Mel. "The people who designed those ranger uniforms knew what they were doing."

Inspector Hudson wished the brim on his own hat were wider.

Übung 35: Wie wird das Wetter? Ordnen Sie die zusammengehörigen Satzhälften richtig zu!

1. The temperature climbed	☐	sunny and mild.
2. The temperature fell	☐	seventy on the coast.
3. The low tonight will be	☐	cloudy and cold.
4. Today's high will be	☐	up to six miles per hour.
5. Winds will be	☐	below freezing.
6. There will be gusts	☐	fifteen degrees.
7. Tomorrow will be	☐	from the south.
8. Tomorrow night will be	☐	into the eighties.

"Maybe this is the time to tell you some stories about hikers who died of dehydration," proposed Bob.
"Please, not now!" cried Susan. "We get the point!"
"I'll save those for later, then," agreed Bob. "How about hikers who died when they wandered off the trail?"
"Thank goodness we have a ranger with us!" exclaimed Inspector Hudson. "I wouldn't have a clue!"
"I'm sure that was a joke, James," said Bob. "It's almost impossible to lose your way on today's trail. But there are others that –."
"Please!" exclaimed Marie. "Tell us tomorrow!"

Übung 36: Schreiben Sie die folgenden Uhrzeiten in Ziffern!

1. It's ten fifteen.	It's ____________.
2. It's half past seven.	It's ____________.
3. It's ten to eight.	It's ____________.
4. It's quarter after six.	It's ____________.

5. It's a quarter to six. It's __________.

6. It's twenty to twelve. It's __________.

The weary hikers put one foot in front of another till they stood once again at the rim of the canyon.
Susan peered over the guard rail.
"You really don't understand just how far down that goes until you've tried it on foot," she said.
"Today's hike was a warm-up exercise," said Ranger Bob, cheerfully. "We like to be sure you're in shape for tomorrow's trails. I'd suggest you soak your feet, lie down for awhile, and maybe spend the rest of the afternoon strolling around the village."
"In my dreams!" said Inspector Hudson. "As you know, it's already evening my time, and I'm beat."
"Have lunch first, and don't sleep through dinner," warned Ranger Bob. "You need to replace calories, and besides, you want to sleep soundly tonight. I'll see you all tomorrow, same time as today."
With a tip of the hat, Ranger Bob was off.

ÜBUNG 37 !

Übung 37: Setzen Sie die richtige Form der Verben ***to lie, to lie*** *oder* ***to lay*** *ein! Achten Sie auf die Zeitform!*

1. ______________ down for a while!

2. You ______________ to me!

3. He usually ______________ down for a nap in the afternoon.

4. She ______________ the baby in his cot.

5. He ______________ about his age.

6. He has been known ____________ about it.

7. Did the hens ____________ eggs today?

8. He ____________ on his back, looking at the stars.

9. Let me ____________ this down on the counter first.

10. The arrowheads had ____________ undiscovered for centuries.

11. I ____________ to him several times.

12. While she ____________ the table, he took a shower.

When the alarm clock rang the next morning, Inspector Hudson was still sleeping.
"Well, I suppose that's one way to cure jet lag," he thought. "Just hike the Grand Canyon the day you arrive. Though of course, if it were any later than three-thirty, I might have awakened of my own accord."
The group assembled once again in the *lobby* and went through their equipment check.
"Today we'll take a shuttle bus to a starting point a bit farther away," said Bob.

This area, too, was paved, but not quite as carefully as the observation area they had started from yesterday. There was a road that curved close to the rim, and a parking lot not far away.
"I think of this as 'Flying Convertible Point'," said Bob.
The hikers snickered, thinking of the final scene of a movie in which two female friends drive around having a grand old time, always one step ahead of trouble. Finally, they know their time is up, and they choose a dramatic exit.

Übung 38: Setzen Sie die richtige Konjunktion ein! ***(and, but, or, so)***

1. Paul __________ Marie are married.
2. Inspector Hudson ordered eggs __________ rashers.
3. He could have ordered pancakes __________ *oatmeal*.
4. He set the alarm for four a.m., __________ he would not miss the tour.
5. Don't forget your socks __________ shoes!
6. I wanted to go with them, __________ I got sick.
7. Do you want your change as a *dollar bill* __________ four *quarters*?
8. Marie wanted a drink, __________ she got out her water bottle.
9. She couldn't decide whether to order chocolate cake __________ ice cream – __________ both!

"People debate whether or not movies or television shows have any effect on a person's *behavior* (behaviour)," said Bob. "I'll let you decide. Let me just say that before that film, there had been altogether four cases of vehicles driven off the rim of Grand Canyon. The year after the home video rental version of that *movie* (film) appeared, we had three cases of suicide by flying vehicle."
It was difficult not to laugh.
"It's a good thing that rental vehicles are well insured," remarked Bob. "They are the vehicle of choice for this mode of 'Death in Grand Canyon'."

"But to be serious for a moment," continued Bob, "it is sobering to think about how determined people can be to end their lives. One of the copycat suicides was committed by a man who had watched that movie over fifty times. He drove out here determined to end it all – and his car got stuck on the rim. He tried to jump, but he landed on a ledge below. Finally, he jumped again, and that was the end."
"That's terrible," said Paul.

Übung 39: Setzen Sie Synonyme aus dem Text ein, um das Lösungswort zu enträtseln!

1. jumped □ _ _ _ _ _
2. earnest _ _ _ _ _ □ _
3. *movie* _ □ _ _
4. imitation _ _ _ _ □ _ _
5. guaranteed □ _ _ _ _ _ _
6. hard □ _ _ _ _ _ _ _ _
7. a total of _ _ _ _ _ □ _ _ _ _

Lösung: _ _ _ _ _ _ _

"Is suicide common at Grand Canyon?" asked Inspector Hudson.
"Not at all," said Bob. "It's easy to imagine putting an end to everything in one romantic leap into the beyond – but remember, most people who commit suicide are extremely depressed. They're not in a condition to start booking a flight to Arizona. Then there's walking out here …"
Bob looked off, and struggled for words.

"There's something else," he said. "I could never prove this, and maybe it's just the ranger in me speaking, but …"
The hikers waited respectfully.
"I think I know what you mean," said Paul. "There's something inspiring about the sight of Grand Canyon."
"It's a healing experience," said Marie.
Bob nodded. "I'd like to think it has inspired some people to live."

ÜBUNG 40 !

Übung 40: Geben Sie den Komparativ und den Superlativ der folgenden Adjektive an!

1. new ______________ ______________
2. fast ______________ ______________
3. small ______________ ______________
4. big ______________ ______________
5. bad ______________ ______________
6. funny ______________ ______________
7. simple ______________ ______________
8. pretty ______________ ______________

The group started down the trail.
"Wow, this is a lot different from the trail we took yesterday," said Paul.
"I thought you'd like to experience a different aspect of the canyon," said Bob. "This is a more heavily-*traveled* (travelled) trail. It follows a *creek* ((stream)), and so there is shade for part of the way."

The hikers knew they would be grateful for the pine trees once the sun was higher. For now, they strode happily along the wide trail, three abreast, as the dawn gently lit up the sky.

"We can walk like this for now," said Bob. "But I have to warn you: mules have the right of way."

Mel stepped out of the way of the evidence that mules did, indeed, carry visitors down into the canyon.

"There's more than one reason to be glad we're wearing boots," Mel remarked.

"It's another way to be sure you're still on the trail," joked Bob. "But seriously, we mark the trails as clearly as we can. And the deaths I'll tell you about first this morning were caused more by people deliberately choosing to stray off the beaten path."

Übung 41: Geben Sie die britische Schreibweise der folgenden Wörter an!

1. *traveling* ________________

2. *signaling* ________________

3. *modeling* ________________

4. *program* ________________

5. *jewelry* ________________

6. *judgment* ________________

7. *argument* ________________

8. *aging* ________________

A good hiking pace is marked by the ability to continue a conversation. The small group clustered together and listened as Bob told story after story of hikers who struck out on their own – and were carried back to their graves. Inspector Hudson looked thoughtful. "Is there a profile," he asked, "of the kind of hiker who is likely to wind up in trouble?"
"He means 'dead'," clarified Marie.

ÜBUNG 42 !

Übung 42: Unterstreichen Sie die inhaltlich nicht dazugehörigen Sätze im folgenden Absatz!

"Absolutely," replied Bob, firmly. He cut his finger. "Our average corpse is a solitary male hiker. The corpse is often cut into pieces. Sheer bravado accounts for some of the deaths. These men – often but not always rather young men – attempt climbs for which they do not have the experience. Are you an experienced typist? No, I was hiking. Some attempt routes for which no amount of experience would be sufficient. She misjudged the difficulty of the trail. They feel the call of the wild – or some such thing – and they leave the marked trail on a fool's errand."
"And the women?" asked Susan. "Does he have this problem, too?"

"I can't say whether women don't feel the same urge to set off into unmarked territory, or whether women simply are more likely to travel with at least one other person. Another person acts as the voice of reason."
"Or it might be," offered Mel, "that a guy alone would take risks that he would never ask another person to take."
"Maybe we're more protective of others than we are of ourselves," agreed Paul. He glanced fondly at Marie.

“Maybe so,” said Bob. “But there is one category of death that is definitely linked to the male sex.” Bob looked a bit embarrassed. “Begging the ladies’ pardon,” he began. “How shall I say this? There seems to be a certain male urge to urinate off a sheer cliff.”
“Well, this certainly would be an A-1 opportunity,” said Susan, in disbelief.
The men all looked embarrassed.

Übung 43: Setzen Sie das richtige der gleich lautenden Wörter ein! ***(there, their, they’re)***

1. ________________ not likely to leave the trail.

2. They had lost ________________ way.

3. The sign warned hikers not to go ________________.

4. ________________ was no chance he was still alive.

5. ________________ experience was limited.

6. Ask if ________________ leaving before dawn!

7. Do they know what ________________ doing?

8. They put on ________________ hiking boots.

“How would you even know that’s what happened?” asked Marie.
“Often, there are witnesses to a fall,” said Bob. “It starts out fine, and then – well, take the case of Lionel Jameson, age 22. He struck a pose out on a rock precipice. It seemed solid enough, but within seconds, the sandstone crumbled beneath his weight. He fell 300 feet to his death.”

"What was he trying to do? Mark the entire Grand Canyon as his territory?" snorted Paul.
"Er, perhaps. There's also the case of young Nelson Garvey, who woke up one night when his family was camping out in the back country. He walked out to the edge, undoubtedly feeling rather sleepy, and seems to have misjudged the distance to the rim."
"With all the water we've been drinking," said Paul, "I can sympathize (sympathise)."
"You might have noticed, though," said Bob, "that most of it evaporates through the skin. It's about time we stopped to tank up on food and water."
"I'm beat," admitted Inspector Hudson.

ÜBUNG 44 !

Übung 44: Bilden Sie die korrekten idiomatischen Vergleiche!

1. as dead	☐ as a feather
2. as dry	☐ as mud
3. as cold	☐ as a fox
4. as light	☐ as a doornail
5. as quick	☐ as a bone
6. as clear	☐ as ice

Though the hikers were tired, it was time to push on. The next rest stop could not come quickly enough.
"I simply cannot believe the amount of water I'm drinking," said Inspector Hudson.
"And we're hiking before the sun is really out," said Paul.
"When the salesperson at the camping goods store showed me this rucksack, I thought it was over the top," said Inspector Hudson. "I had been thinking of a rucksack as a canvas bag of sorts for carry-

ing an extra jacket, not a plastic bag for carrying water! And it seemed a bit ridiculous, to be biting on a plastic tube to drink."
"It's the best thing you could have bought," said Mel. "That way, you don't even have to stop to drink."
"On a really hot day, on an exposed trail, a hiker needs two gallons of water a day," confirmed Bob.
"That's a lot of water!" cried Marie.

Übung 45: Setzen Sie die richtige Mengenangabe ein! Die folgenden Wörter können auch mehrfach verwendet werden.
(much, many, a lot, a little, a few, few, most)

1. I don't save ____________ money.
2. I don't save ____________ of money.
3. Might I have ____________ of your ice cream?
4. Not ____________ people travel this way any more.
5. ____________ people still use fountain pens.
6. ____________ people feel more at home speaking their native language.
7. ____________ people respond well to being called a fool.
8. Would you pass me ____________ of those paper clips?

"If people don't have enough water, they die," said Bob.
"Don't the rangers carry extra water for emergencies?" asked Mel.
"We have some," asserted Bob. "But we're not here to hand out lemonade. I'm carrying other equipment, as well."

"Such as?"
"A rope," said Bob, grimly. "A spike. A hammer. A first aid kit that's a little bigger than yours."
No one spoke. They hadn't realised ((realized)) that Bob's rucksack was heavier than theirs. His practised (*practiced*) gait made hiking seem so easy.
"If someone gets dehydrated on the trail," said Bob, "what they usually need is intravenous fluids. Now, let's take a rest while I explain."
Everyone drank up.

ÜBUNG 46 !

Übung 46: Sie wurden unterbrochen! Setzen Sie die richtigen Vergangenheitsformen der Verben ein!

1. I (write) ____________ when he came in.
2. She (sing) ____________ until he asked her to stop.
3. They (hike) ______________ on that trail as soon as the sun was up.
4. She (put away) ______________ the groceries when the phone (ring) ____________.
5. Sally (do) ____________________ very well until she (get) ____________ the news that her dog had died.
6. George (play) ____________ in the sandbox when his mother (call) ____________.

7. We (be sure) ________________ we would win, until Roger (score) ______________ a goal.

"The signs of dehydration include light-headedness and, unfortunately, disinterest in food or water. People no longer even feel thirsty, and they forget to make themselves drink. Core body temperature rises to 105 or 106 degrees, and they lose the ability to think straight."
"I guess this is where being alone gets really dangerous," remembered Paul.
"That's right," said Bob. "There's no one else there to tell the person to stop, drink and signal for help."
"I'll bet guys make some bad choices in that state," guessed Mel.
Bob nodded. "*Whoa*! ((Stop!))" he cried. "Everybody up! Here come the mules!"

Übung 47: Was bedeutet das „tierische" Idiom?

ÜBUNG 47 !

1. He's as stubborn as a mule.
   a) ☐ He is unwilling to change his mind.
   b) ☐ He is very loyal.

2. It's two miles, as the crow flies.
   a) ☐ It takes only ten minutes to get there.
   b) ☐ It's two miles away, but you probably can't get there directly.

3. Don't let the cat out of the bag!
   a) ☐ Don't start trouble!
   b) ☐ Don't tell the secret!

4. There's no room to swing a cat.
   a) ☐ The space is not big enough to flog a British sailor.
   b) ☐ The job is impossible.

5. I worked as a dogsbody.
   a) ☐ I fed the animals in the veterinary clinic.
   b) ☐ I did all the worst jobs.

6. That candidate was a dark horse.
   a) ☐ He resembled the famous racehorse, Secretariat.
   b) ☐ Nobody thought he would win.

7. Let sleeping dogs lie!
   a) ☐ Don't be cruel to animals!
   b) ☐ Don't stir up trouble!

8. She's a snake in the grass.
   a) ☐ She's a person who cannot be trusted.
   b) ☐ She moves silently.

He reminded them to be sure to face the animals. "It happened once that a mule train passed some hikers on a narrow rock ledge. One of the hikers turned his *pack* towards the animals. A mule caught the *pack* on its way past, and the hiker was tossed to his death."
"Some of those stretches are pretty narrow," said Mel, with concern. "Mules have a reputation for being *ornery* ((nasty)), too. Do the riders ever fall off?"
"We advise people not to sign up for a mule ride if they are afraid of heights," said Bob, earnestly.
Inspector Hudson laughed out loud. "Here you are, looking down three thousand feet to the Colorado River, and your problem is that your feet are three feet off the ground?"

Übung 48: Unterstreichen Sie jeweils das größte Element der Gruppe!

ÜBUNG 48 !

1. donkey, mule, dog, coyote
2. thousand, dozen, billion, hundred
3. ton, pound, ounce, hundredweight
4. teaspoon, drop, tablespoon, half-pint
5. island, promontory, continent, precipice
6. walk, journey, hike, meander

"It's a matter of perspective," sighed Bob. "The river is three thousand feet away, but those three thousand feet have nothing to do with you. Your feet – well, they belong to you. And they're supposed to be on the ground."
The animals trudged by, and their riders waved gaily. It was still early in the morning, and everyone was in a good mood.
"We'd better get going ourselves," advised Bob.
The hikers made good time on the pleasant trail, stopping dutifully as morning brightened the sky. Soon they left the water and shade behind, advancing again into the world of carved rock and unrelenting sun.

Übung 49: Setzen Sie ***good*** *oder* ***well*** *ein!*

ÜBUNG 49 !

1. That was a ________________ story!
2. I don't feel very ________________.
3. It will do you ________________ to go on holiday.
4. I'm doing ________________, thank you.

5. Isn't he feeling ______________?

6. It's just as ______________ he couldn't come.

7. It's not ______________ to travel when you're sick.

8. I'm not very ______________ at arithmetic.

9. Leave ______________ enough alone!

10. The coffee smells ______________ .

11. He ate ______________ at the restaurant.

At last they stopped on an outcrop of rock with a staggering view over Grand Canyon.
"I can't get over the *colors*," murmured Paul.
"I always wanted to go to Mars," said Susan.
"Mars?" wondered Inspector Hudson.
"Mars," said Susan, firmly. "My dream was to be an astronaut. I didn't give too much thought to the flying part. I just wanted to be a citizen of the red planet."
"This comes awfully close," agreed Inspector Hudson. "I've done a lot of hiking in the Lake District, but England is nothing like this."
The group laughed, and Inspector Hudson laughed, too.
"Isn't that Wordsworth country?" asked Paul. "I remember reading his poetry in school: 'A host of golden daffodils'."
The group was giddy with laughter.
"This landscape would require a different sort of writer altogether," agreed Inspector Hudson. "A different sort of mind."
"Someone fierce," said Susan. "As fierce as death."
"You'd all better drink up," advised Ranger Bob. "I'm afraid you're losing it."

Übung 50: Übersetzen Sie und formulieren Sie dabei eine höfliche Absage!

1. I'm afraid I can't (kommen) ________________ this evening.
2. I'm afraid I must (bleiben) ________________ at home.
3. I'm afraid you (sein) ________________ too clever for me.
4. I'd rather not (reisen) ________________ to Chicago.
5. I'd rather not (riskieren) ________________ a relapse.
6. I'd rather not (belästigen) ________________ you with such a minor problem.

At last they reached their turning point for the day. Because today's hike was longer, they had brought tinned (*canned*) food that would not spoil in the heat.

"My water's lukewarm," complained Marie.

"This objection has been known to kill," observed Ranger Bob.

"Don't you ever let up?" she exclaimed.

"'Death in Grand Canyon' is more than a catchy name for a tour," replied Bob. "Every year, the rangers respond to 400 medical emergencies, and there are 250 medical evacuations from the canyon."

Mel whistled. "That must cost taxpayers a fortune."

"It is charged to the person we evacuate," said Bob. "A helicopter evacuation costs about two thousand dollars."

"That must be the best way out of here," said Paul.

"The problem is that it's a high-risk operation for the rescue team," said Mel. "It must be hard lifting off at this altitude, and the winds in the canyon must be unpredictable."

"You seem to know a lot about helicopters," observed Inspector Hudson, attentively.

Übung 51: Ordnen Sie die Buchstaben zu einem sinnvollen Wort!

"He's right, though," (1. niocfrdem) ______________ Bob. "And there are many times when we can only get to the person by foot. In fact, we always send out search and (2. scuree) ______________ teams by foot. They are the most (3. efctfeiev) ______________ form of help. I remember a case where two rangers *rappeled* (rappelled) down on ropes to reach a (4. krehi) ______________ who had fallen to a ledge below the trail. It was winter, and his body (5. peartmeuter) ______________ had fallen so low that he was no longer even (6. vhisenirg) ______________. The rangers hooked up an intravenous fluid supply and stayed with the (7. jnrudie) ______________ hiker all night, keeping him warm with their own body heat until a (8. phteeolicr) ______________ could fly in the next morning."

"You rangers are pretty brave," said Mel.
"Men and women both," said the ranger, tipping his hat unconsciously.
On the way back up, they stopped at several rocky precipices. The kaleidoscopic colours of Grand Canyon performed a slow, endless dance. The spectacle was accompanied by shifting breezes.
"It's not just the sight of it, is it?" said Susan. "It's the whole experience… It's overwhelming."

"Out here, one really feels part of this world," agreed Inspector Hudson. "It's hard to go back."
"I would have no argument with my bed right now," Marie countered.
By the time they were back in the shady beginning of the trail, they were grateful indeed for the relief from the sun. The happy babbling of the brook kept them company in the final stretch of their day's hike. They were glad to be deposited back at the lodge at last.

Übung 52: Wählen Sie den Satz mit der richtigen Wortfolge!

1. a) ☐ On Mondays, she goes to English classes at the Peachtree School.
   b) ☐ She goes to the Peachtree School on Monday to English classes.
   c) ☐ Either a) or b).

2. a) ☐ Mike signed a contract to rent a beach house next summer.
   b) ☐ Mike signed a contract next summer to rent a beach house.
   c) ☐ Either a) or b).

3. a) ☐ Carefully smooth the plaster with quick, even strokes.
   b) ☐ Smooth the plaster carefully with quick, even strokes.
   c) ☐ Either a) or b).

4. a) ☐ He usually goes to the gym around the corner.
   b) ☐ He goes to the gym around the corner usually.
   c) ☐ Either A or B.

5. a) ☐ I often think it would be better to get it over with quickly.
   b) ☐ I think it would be better to quickly get it over with often.
   c) + Either a) or b)

6. a) ☐ An old blue car drove slowly down the winding road.
   b) ☐ Down the winding road drove slowly an old blue car.
   c) ☐ Either a) or b).

RRRRRRRrrrrrrrrrrrrrinnnnnnnggggggggggg!!!
"Goodness gracious," moaned Inspector Hudson. "Can it be that time already?" The advantage of jet lag was wearing off.
The other hikers also looked a bit *peaked* ((weary)) at breakfast. Even Mel, the strongest of the group, looked the worse for wear.
"Are you feeling a bit under the weather, Mel?" asked Inspector Hudson.
"He couldn't sleep last night," said Susan.
"I slept like a log," said Marie.
"I hit the sack, and that was it for me," admitted Paul.
"I was out like a light, myself," confirmed Inspector Hudson.
Mel shifted uncomfortably in his seat and looked out the window at the moonlit canyon.
"We'd better get moving," said Susan. "We don't want to keep Ranger Bob waiting. We have to catch the van to Lookout Point."

ÜBUNG 53 !

Übung 53: Was bedeutet das Idiom? Kreuzen Sie die richtige Umschreibung an!

1. I slept off a hangover.
   a) ☐ I slept under the cliff.
   b) ☐ I got rid of a hangover by sleeping.

2. She slept in on Saturday.
   a) ☐ She deliberately slept late on Saturday.
   b) ☐ She slept at her own house on Saturday.

3. My foot went to sleep!
   a) ☐ I stepped on my dance partner's foot.
   b) ☐ My foot feels numb.

4. He's made his own bed, and now he can lie in it.
   a) ☐ I don't care, because he created this problem for himself.
   b) ☐ A soldier can be happy that he has a tent.

5. I'd like to sleep on it before deciding.
   a) ☐ I won't marry you until I'm sure you're the princess.
   b) ☐ I need at least a day to decide.

6. She put her dog to sleep.
   a) ☐ She had her dog killed by the veterinarian.
   b) ☐ She tucked her dog into his bed.

Once they were settled in the van, Ranger Bob told them about the trail they would hike today.
"We're driving out to a more remote location, from which we will have an excellent view of different layers of rock."
He paused briefly and then went on with his explanations.

"You will be able to identify several layers of limestone and sandstone *toward* (towards) the rim."
"We saw several different *colors* yesterday," remembered Paul. "It was amazing."
"The canyon looks like striped ribbon," smiled Susan.

"That's what makes it easy to study geology here," agreed Ranger Bob. "The history of the planet is laid out before your eyes."
"I hear the evidence goes back two billion years," said Mel.
"Two billion years ago, Grand Canyon lay under an ancient sea," confirmed Bob. "Grand Canyon offers a view of some of the oldest rocks on the surface of the earth."
"When you say 'billion'," asked Inspector Hudson, "do you mean a *US billion* or a British billion?"

ÜBUNG 54 !

Übung 54: US billion oder British billion? Setzen Sie die Wörter in die richtige Reihenfolge!

1. a US is the ninth billion power ten to

____

2. US billion that that zeroes a means has nine

____

3. twelve billion has a British zeroes

____

4. million billion thousand a is US a

____

5. a British is a million billion million

____

6. equal British US trillion a billion is to a

____

7. in fact, US use most today the Britons standard

____

8. who care people of the Inspector is Hudson one few

____

"I mean a *US billion,* James," replied Bob. "A thousand million. In other words, so long ago that most of us can't imagine it, *period* (full stop)."
Marie rolled her eyes.
"Down at the bottom of the Canyon, the Colorado River is now working its way through a pinkish granite rock layer. That rock is much harder than the rock up here at the rim, so the rate of erosion is much slower now than in previous eras. You'll see how soft the rock at the top is," continued Ranger Bob. "It crumbles. That's why I'm asking you to be very careful this morning, and to stay away from the edge."
Finally, they arrived at the head of the trail.
"Wow! I have got to get some pictures of this!" exclaimed Paul.
They all took photographs, and started off down the trail.

*Übung 55: Vervollständigen Sie die folgenden Sätze mit der richtigen Form von **get**!*

ÜBUNG 55 !

1. Did you ______________ the newspaper this morning?

2. You're ______________ on my nerves.

3. I plan to ______________ rid of my old car soon.

4. I ______________ something in my eye.

5. One can see that he's ____________ old.

6. How are you ____________ home from the party?

7. I hope the baby doesn't ____________ the measles!

8. I've ____________ the flu.

"This has been the most spectacular view so far," said Paul, as they paused to rest. "The cliffs are unbelievable."

"The layers you told us about are unmistakable," said Susan, looking out over the canyon. "The drop-offs certainly are dramatic!"

"Maybe it's time to tell the story of another jumper," said Ranger Bob. "This is a case of 'Death in Grand Canyon' that is especially hard to understand.

Ronald Berger started out on the wrong foot, *for sure* ((without a doubt)). He headed off into the canyon carrying only a *styrofoam* (polystyrene) coffee cup full of water."

Even Marie stared in disbelief. "*Are you kidding me*? ((You can't be serious!))"

Ranger Bob nodded.

"*We know for sure* ((We are certain)), because people coming out of the canyon told us they had met a young man, hiking alone, who asked them for water. He was carrying an eight-ounce *styrofoam* cup with a plastic lid."

"Well, in that case, I guess it was okay," smirked Mel.

ÜBUNG 56 !

Übung 56: Ergänzen Sie die fehlenden Buchstaben!

1. st _ r _ fo _ m

2. pan _ r _ m _

3. pr _ m _ nt _ r _

4. _ m _ rg _ nc _ _ s

5. m _ _ sles

6. d _ h _ dr _ tion

7. intr _ v _ n _ _ s

"We knew right away that we'd better start looking. We posted rangers at the head of the trail. They questioned everyone coming back up. Sure enough, several hikers had given water to *Mr.* Berger.

The reports tapered off. We knew he must be in trouble, but we still couldn't find him. We did locate the spot where the last hiker reported giving him water. That hiker told us that while *Mr.* Berger had no water, he did have a detailed map of the area.

Not far from that spot, an unmarked trail branched off and headed downhill. We feared that he had decided to head for the river."

"There are warnings posted everywhere, advising people not to hike on trails that are not maintained by the National Park Service," remarked Susan.

"Remember what I was saying yesterday," Bob reminded them. "Dehydration and bad decisions go together, and the people most at risk are solo males."

Übung 57: Verbinden Sie die zusammengehörigen Satzhälften! Setzen Sie die richtige Ziffer ein!

1. "My goodness!"	☐ he asked.
2. "Is it true?"	☐ they shouted.

3. "What time is it?"	☐ she asserted.
4. "Our team won!"	☐ he gasped.
5. "Yes,"	☐ she wondered.
6. "No, sir,"	☐ he said.

"We suspected that *Mr.* Berger had seen a waterfall marked on his map," continued Ranger Bob. "It's not far, but the problem is that the water flows only in the spring. This was July.

When the rangers got to the waterfall, they were greeted by a strange and terrible sight. It seems *Mr.* Berger had carefully taken off his hat, his shoes, and his lightweight *backpack*, and thrown them down the dry wall of the waterfall."

"Maybe he was trying to judge the distance," said Mel.

"Maybe so," said Bob. "Or maybe he was delirious. At any rate, he could see a tiny pool of water that had not yet evaporated, thirty feet below. And he went for it."

"He jumped?" asked Susan, horrified.

"I'm afraid so," said Ranger Bob, tipping his hat unconsciously.

Mel looked agitated. "He jumped? Just like that?"

"It was the only way down. He jumped," said Bob, "holding his *styrofoam* cup."

ÜBUNG 58 !

Übung 58: Sind die folgenden Ausdrücke britisch, amerikanisch oder beides?

1. luggage __________
2. baggage __________
3. suitcase __________
4. knapsack __________

5. rucksack ______________________

6. backpack ______________________

7. styrofoam ______________________

8. cup ______________________

"I hope you didn't get too upset by that story," said Bob. "We have to pull ourselves together for the next stretch."

The little group set out on the trail. At one point, they met two rangers who were repairing a sign.

"Good morning," said Inspector Hudson, politely.

"*Howdy*," said the first ranger, as she turned to greet them.

"*Howdy*," said the second ranger, touching his fingers to his broad-brimmed hat.

"You're out early," said Mel.

"We like to get an early start," said the first ranger.

The little group hiked along, all alone in the splendour (*splendor*) of Grand Canyon.

"This is so beautiful, I feel like I'm walking on air," exclaimed Marie.

No one felt tired any more. Their spirits were buoyed up by the sight of the far reaches of the canyon. Skirting the edges of the cliffs was exhilarating.

At last they came to a promontory that extended out over the vastness of Grand Canyon.

"I can't believe my eyes," said Paul. "It's like paradise." He got out his camera, and everyone followed suit. They knew that photos could never do justice to the panorama, but they each wanted to take with them a little piece of paradise.

"Of all the views of Grand Canyon, this is the one I love the best," said Ranger Bob. He shaded his eyes and gazed into the distance.

A horrible scream tore through the air. The hikers looked frantically about.
Susan was over the edge!
"Help! Help!" shouted Paul.
"Save her!" cried Marie.
"Susan!" yelled Mel Gordon.
Inspector Hudson stared in horror, as Ranger Bob ordered, "Stand back! This ledge could crumble any second!"

ÜBUNG 59 !

Übung 59: Unterstreichen Sie im nächsten Abschnitt die acht Verben im Simple Past!

Over and over she rolled. The slope was steep, but it was not an open fall. Down and down she went. Each time she turned, she grabbed at the rock of the canyon wall.
The sandstone of the Grand Canyon broke off in her hands.
"Mel!" she screamed. "Mel!"

The broken rock fell with her. All around, she heard nothing but the sound of falling rock, tumbling, tumbling down.
As she fell, she saw the colours of the great desert. First the sky, then the cliffs, then the canyon depths, and once again, the rock of the canyon wall. The colours whirled over and over, in a beautiful blur. A bit of blue and white, every shade of sunset orange, the darkening floor of the canyon below, the lighter brown of the canyon wall.
Blue, yellow, orange – darkness. The colours whirled around like a picture postcard turned into a nightmare.
"Mel!" she screamed. "Mel!"
She fell through a space that was no space, and a time that was no

time. There was nothing at all, only the falling.

And the fight to live.

Susan was a fighter.

She fought to grab anything that would break her fall. Any rock, any pebble, any –

Tree!

A tiny desert pine tree had worked its roots into the wall of the canyon. Susan landed face down, right on the tree.

Übung 60: Unterstreichen Sie die Partizipialkonstruktionen im folgenden Absatz!

ÜBUNG 60 !

Breathing hard, she almost cried with happiness.

"What luck!" she thought, laughing at herself. Two minutes ago, her standards for luck had been a bit higher.

"Here I am, lying on a baby pine tree, hanging over the – Don't even think about it," she told herself. "Just breathe."

The needles of the pine tree, adapted to the harsh climate, were thin and sharp. They cut into Susan's skin.

"The needles help the tree to survive here. This tree is a survivor, and so am I."

Hanging on to the needles, Susan thought, "Just breathe."

Thinking only of balancing her body, Susan took slow, shallow breaths.

"Good," she thought. "So far, so good."

A creaking sound came from the tree. She felt her body move.

"I didn't move," she thought. "I didn't. This can't be right."

She felt the movement again.

"Oh, no," she realised. "The tree!"

The roots of the tree were not very deep. It was just a young tree that had made a spot for itself in a very unlikely place.
"Like me," thought Susan. "I'm not supposed to be here, either. I was standing there, and – No! Don't think that way!"
Susan risked a glance to her left. The magnificent sight of the Grand Canyon opened out before her, as few human beings would ever see it.
A great joy filled Susan's heart. She felt a great urge to look out into the – "No!" she thought. "No!"
Susan gripped the tree and breathed slowly to centre (*center*) her thoughts. She tried to look only at the canyon wall.
"Just look at the wall, Susan. Turn your head to the wall."

ÜBUNG 61 !

Übung 61: Geben Sie die (eher) amerikanische Schreibweise der folgenden Wörter an!

1. realise ____________________
2. organise ____________________
3. surprise ____________________
4. dialogue ____________________
5. analogue ____________________
6. catalogue ____________________
7. cheque ____________________

The calm voice of Ranger Bob came down to her from the rim of the Grand Canyon. It was only a hundred feet above her head. It wasn't even straight up.

"Keeping looking at the wall. That's right."
Susan heard voices that seemed to come from another world. She heard Marie screaming and shouting, "Get out the rope! Hurry! Hurry!"
Susan closed her eyes. She wanted to scream, too.
"Hold on to the tree, Susan. Just hold on. You're doing fine."
Susan's body shook just a bit, and she heard the little tree groan. A few small pebbles broke off from the rock. She heard them roll away for a second or two, and then – nothing at all.
"Hang on there, Susan," said the ranger. "Remain calm. We're on our way to get you. Can you talk to me?"
Susan heard a strange, shaking sound. She felt her voice in her chest, but no words came out. It made no sense. Nothing made any sense at all.
"We're very close," she heard him say. But Ranger Bob sounded very far away.

Übung 62: Unterstreichen Sie im folgenden Absatz Susans Gedanken!

Another voice spoke to her.
"This voice was very different. That English person – what was his name again?"
"This is Inspector Hudson, Susan. James Hudson. Remember me?"
Susan nodded her head.
"That strange accent," she thought. "What is he doing here? What am I doing here?"
Then she remembered where 'here' was:
"I am over the edge of the Grand Canyon."
"Splendid!" said Inspector Hudson, calmly. "You are doing very well, Susan!"

"For someone who is about to –," she thought.
"Don't think about anything but my voice," he continued.
"His voice is beautiful. I have always wanted to go to London. Maybe everything will be fine. I could *take a vacation* (go on holiday). I could go to London."
"Inspector Hudson!" she called. "James!"
"But the words came out wrong. Everything is wrong."

"That's right. You are doing very well," he repeated. "Just hold on, now."
Susan felt her hands slip on the little tree. Even in the dry desert air, the palms of her hands were wet.
"Hold on, Susan."
In the background, she heard people shouting. Her husband was shouting. Suddenly she remembered.
"Get Mel!" she cried. "Get Mel!"
Marie's voice came down. "She wants her husband!"
"Get Mel!"
"Susan?"
"That lovely English voice again."
"I want you to do something for me. You must do it very, very slowly. Don't move until you understand exactly what you must do."
Susan waited.

ÜBUNG 63 !

Übung 63: Formulieren Sie die folgenden Sätze im Imperativ! Verwenden Sie die Kurzform, wo möglich!

1. (put) ____________________ that down!

2. Please (wait) __________________ until Sam is ready!

3. (eat) ________________ your vegetables!

4. (tell) ____________ Dr (*Dr.*) Smith to come immediately!

5. (not move) ________________, or I'll shoot!

6. Please (not wait) ________________ for me!

7. (not think) ________________ I didn't hear that!

8. (not try) ________________ to tell me you didn't know!

"You are on a tree, isn't that right?"
"It's not so bad," she thought. "Maybe it's not so bad."
"You're going to be alright, Susan. Just underneath you is a ledge."
She listened.
"If you can put your foot out, your body weight will rest on both the tree and the ledge. That will be more secure. It will only be for a few minutes. We are coming to get you."
"I'm not moving one inch," thought Susan. She held the tree even tighter.

Suddenly a tree branch snapped.
The Englishman's voice came down to her again.
"Put your right foot out behind you, very slowly. It will come down on a ledge. Keep holding on to the tree."
Very carefully, she stretched out her foot. It hung in the open air.
"The ledge is right under you, Susan. You must step down onto your right foot."

Susan tried to think of anything else she could possibly do. She wanted so much just to hold the tree.
The little tree sighed and cracked.

Übung 64: ***Look, see*** *oder* ***watch****? Verknüpfen Sie die zusammengehörigen Satzhälften und tragen Sie die richtige Ziffer in das Kästchen ein!*

1. Cats can see	☐	for a long time.
2. Watch	☐	you later!
3. He was looking	☐	in the dark.
4. See	☐	television.
5. She had not seen him	☐	what you're doing!
6. I like to watch	☐	for her.

"I hope that English person knows what he's talking about," she thought.

"I can see the ledge right behind you, Susan. Come on, now. Right foot down."

"What's the alternative?" she asked herself.

She stepped back. As her weight shifted, the little tree broke.

"Stand on the ledge, Susan!" cried Ranger Bob. "Don't move! Hold the tree for luck, but don't lean on it!"

"Look at the tree roots, Susan," said Inspector Hudson, in his calm, steady voice. "Stick tight to the canyon wall, Susan, just like that tree."

She smiled just a little and fixed her eyes on the miniature world of the canyon wall.

"The rock is layered in many thin stripes. It is interesting. How did sand become rock? How many millions of years did it take? And how hard must a little seed work to send roots right into the rock wall? The rock here wasn't that hard, was it? It was always crumbling off when I – No! Don't think that!"

She screamed as a few pebbles tore loose and fell.

"Where did they fall?" she wondered.

"We're coming to get you," said Inspector Hudson, just loud enough for her to hear.

Übung 65: Setzen Sie das Verb in die richtige Form des Present Tense!

1. I (go) ________________ to the store to buy milk.
2. I (go) ________________ to the store every day.
3. We (go) ________________ to London on holiday.
4. He (go) ________________ to lose his temper.
5. She (think) ________________ about applying to university.
6. Her mother (think) ________________ it is a good idea.
7. Her cousins (say) ________________ they are not so sure.
8. We (try) ________________ to do the right thing.

Inspector Hudson was not afraid. She, Susan, was not afraid. She took her first big, easy breath. She felt wonderfully calm.
"The pebbles fall into the canyon," she thought. "Into the beautiful world of the Grand Canyon."
Susan remembered the sunset, and the colours, and the vast, eternal space. She remembered her fall, but without the pain. Susan remembered everything. In her mind, she saw the Grand Canyon stretch out before her, calling to her.
"Ranger Bob is about to come down on a rope," said Inspector Hudson, somewhat more urgently. "He'll bring you back, Susan. Just hang on, there."

She heard the clattering sound of a man rappelling (*rappeling*) down the face of the canyon wall. The rock broke all around him, and the pebbles skipped over her like a meteor shower.

"Get me?" thought Susan. "Back?"

Susan turned her face to the vast, open space.

She followed her eyes.

"No!" screamed the people on the rim. "Susan, no!"

ÜBUNG 66 !

*Übung 66: Vervollständigen Sie die folgenden Sätze mit **two, too, to** oder **into**!*

Ranger Bob bounced down the last few feet. In 1. ________ seconds, he was standing where Susan had stood.

Bob, 2. ________, stared 3. ________ space.

The only sound came from the last of the pebbles Bob had kicked loose on his rapid descent 4. ________ save Susan. Each pebble rattled and clattered down 5. ________ where Bob stood.

And then, nothing.

Ignoring his own advice, Bob, 6. ________, stared out over the canyon. There was nothing 7. ________ see.

Marie cried softly.

Bob tugged on the rope. "I'm coming up," he said.

Ranger Bob climbed hand over hand, setting his boots 8. ________ the sandstone so that he stood out from the wall.

Pebbles scattered down and away, and no one cared any more. Silently, Inspector Hudson helped Ranger Bob to climb up over the edge.
"It's alright, everybody," Bob said, rather pointlessly. "Please stand back from the edge."
The group followed Bob back to a big rock away from the edge of the canyon. Bob sat down heavily on a smaller rock.
"I'm really sorry about Susan," he said.
"You can't just leave her there!" shouted Mel. "What if she's on the next ledge, just below?"
"There is no ledge below the one we can see," said Ranger Bob. "There's nothing at all; just blue sky and Grand Canyon. It's a 500-foot drop to the next place where her body could possibly be."
"How do you know?" accused Mel.
Bob raised his head. "I know because someone else fell off this cliff four years and two months ago."
"It was in all the papers," said Marie, softly.

Übung 67: Bringen Sie die Sätze in die richtige Reihenfolge!

ÜBUNG 67 !

1. Mel calm looked strangely Gordon

____

2. "please yourselves blame don't," said Bob

____

3. group Hudson at the member looked each Inspector of

____

4. Susan he crying remembered out

5. Bob's bravery remembered he

6. get crumbling rappelled (*rappeled*) rock he down the to her

7. had earth what on happened

8. jump did why she

9. "saw we all it," said Paul

10. "we her jump saw"

Just then two rangers ran up, breathless. "We got your call," they panted.
One look told them all they needed to know.
"She's gone," said Bob.
"Let's call it in," said one of the new rangers. "'Search and Rescue' has a helicopter on the way."
"Have we got a next of kin?" asked the second ranger.
"I'm her husband," said Mel, stepping forward.
"I'm very sorry, sir."
The female ranger turned to the group.

"We know *you folks* ((you)) feel pretty awful right about now," said the ranger. "It's a terrible thing."
The ranger sighed.
"I'm afraid we have to ask you to stay close by," she continued. "The police will want to talk to each of you individually, to ask exactly what you saw."

Übung 68: Setzen Sie ein Komma, wo nötig!

ÜBUNG 68 !

1. Ranger Bob called them because Susan went over the edge.
2. Because it was an emergency the rangers came on the double.
3. Although it had happened years ago she still remembered.
4. Even though he was short on money he insisted on paying.
5. Marie is safe above whereas Susan is in big trouble.
6. I jumped because she dared me to do it.

"She jumped!" exclaimed Marie. "What else do you want to know?"
"We all saw it," agreed Paul.
"I understand," said the ranger, calmly. "And I know it seems simple. But I must ask you, please, not to discuss it among yourselves until after the Park Police have taken your statements."
"Don't you have any decency?" Marie burst out. "This poor man's wife just died!"
Inspector Hudson tried to soothe Marie. "It's a matter of routine," he said. "Just come along, now."
By the time they had hiked up the remaining trail, there were police cars waiting to take them to the Park Police Station for questioning. A small crowd of hikers had gathered in the parking lot, straining to see what was going on there.

"This is just like in the movies!" exclaimed one hiker.
"Please, sir," asked a police officer. "Stand back."
The five remaining members of the group were escorted to police cars. The lead car pulled out, and away they drove.

*Übung 69: Vervollständigen Sie die folgende Sätze mit **to** oder **towards**!*

1. Inspector Hudson talked calmly __________ Susan.
2. The hikers were brought __________ the police cars.
3. The spectators walked __________ the police cars, but were told to stay away.
4. They wanted to get __________ the suspects, but the police did not allow it.
5. If you walk __________ the big tree, you will see the trail just before you get there.
6. The teacher urged us to act with charity __________ our fellow citizens.
7. If you get __________ London before me, please tell Mary I'm on my way.

At the Park Police Station, the officers were polite but distant. It seemed this was not the first time they had dealt with death in Grand Canyon.
Each of the hikers, including Ranger Bob, was interviewed separately and asked to give an initial account of the incident.

A grey-haired Park Police officer motioned to Inspector Hudson. "I'm Captain Harvey of the Park Police. Would you mind coming with me to answer a few follow-up questions?"
Inspector Hudson followed him into a simply-furnished room and sat across the desk from Captain Harvey.
"Inspector James Hudson?"
The police officer looked again at the business card in his hand. "Of Scotland Yard?"
"Yes," answered Inspector Hudson, simply.

Übung 70: Setzen Sie das passende Hilfsverb ein!
(can, could, may, might, would)

1. __________ you touch your toes?
2. __________ Jonathan reach Greg on the phone yesterday?
3. __________ I be excused?
4. __________ you see the tower in the distance now?
5. I __________ go to the party later, if I decide to take a break.
6. I'd like to take your picture, if I __________.
7. I'm not sure he __________ do it, even if he tried.
8. I __________ not annoy the dog, if I were you.

"What are you doing here, if I may ask?"
"I'm on holiday," answered Inspector Hudson.
"And to take a break from Scotland Yard, you booked a tour on 'Death in Grand Canyon'?"

"Correct," he nodded.

The police officer leant (*leaned*) across his desk.

"You wouldn't happen to be a bit too fascinated with murder, would you, Inspector Hudson?"

"My interest is strictly professional, sir," replied Inspector Hudson. "And if I can be of any service in this matter, I would be delighted to help with the investigation."

"We don't need any help from Scotland Yard," Captain Harvey snapped. "We're doing just fine without you. This is a cut-and-dried, all-American suicide."

ÜBUNG 71

Übung 71: Ordnen Sie die zusammengehörigen Satzhälften mit ***can, could, is able to*** *richtig zu! Schreiben Sie die entsprechende Ziffer in das Kästchen!*

1. I'm sure he could do it	☐ play the piano.
2. I can	☐ to lift very heavy boxes.
3. He is able	☐ already read when I was four.
4. I could	☐ tell me the time, please?
5. Can you	☐ if he tried.
6. Could you	☐ touch your toes?

The police officer shuffled some papers on the desk.

"Three people have just told me that they saw the decedent jump off the ledge, just as Ranger Bob Snyder was *rappeling* (rappelling) down to get her. That's three eyewitnesses, Inspector Hudson. They all say they saw it with their own eyes."

"I'm sure they did," said Inspector Hudson, agreeably. "I, too, saw her jump to her death from the ledge about a hundred feet below the rim."

"Open-and-shut case," repeated the Captain.
"Well, the eyewitnesses say they saw her jump from the ledge," mused Hudson. "But what about the fall from the rim to the ledge?"
The police officer looked at Hudson suspiciously.

Übung 72: Unterstreichen Sie das richtige der gleich klingenden Wörter!

1. Be sure to water the flower/flour!
2. The guest did not mean to brake/break the glass.
3. The symbol of the rangers is a bare/bear wearing a broad-brimmed hat.
4. Please clothes/close the door!
5. She took a moment to weigh/way the alternatives.
6. It took place during the reign/rain of Queen Victoria.
7. Which/witch/ which/witch/ is which/witch?

"Something I learnt on the tour," said Hudson, "is that there are surprisingly few suicides in Grand Canyon. It takes a considerable amount of planning to carry out a suicide; most people who feel they cannot go on with life also lack the energy to plan a trip to Grand Canyon."
Captain Harvey drummed his fingernails on the worn wooden desk.
"Susan, on the other hand," continued Hudson, "had just competently and cheerfully – and in the company of five other people – carried out a three-day hike."
"Hrrrmph," said the Captain.

Übung 73: Finden Sie die entsprechenden Adverbien und enträtseln Sie das Lösungswort!

1. In a happy manner

_ _ _ _ □ _ _ _ _ _

2. In an unhappy manner

_ □ _ _ _

3. In a professional manner

_ _ _ _ _ _ □ _ _ _ _

4. In a cooperative manner

_ □ _ _ _ _ _ _ _

5. In an unexpected manner

_ _ □ _ _ _ _ _ _ _ _

6. In an untrusting manner

_ _ □ _ _ _ _ _ _ _ _ _

Lösung: _ _ _ _ _ _ _

"Another thing," added Hudson. "Several of Susan's remarks over the past two and a half days suggested that she had a strange relationship to the canyon. She seemed both afraid of and drawn to the great heights. At one point, she even refused to go on. Now, it may be that at the edge today, she panicked and fell. But I would think that someone who is afraid of heights would choose some other way of committing suicide."

"But she jumped, just the same," repeated Captain Harvey.

"She did," agreed Hudson, "as far as we could tell from a distance of one hundred feet. But that was only the second part of the fall. We haven't yet established what happened before that. What about the first part, at the edge of the trail?"

"How about: she jumped?" asked the Captain, impatiently.

"It's possible, but not necessary," persisted Hudson. "What if she had been pushed?"
Hudson looked out the window into the far distance.
"Susan fought for her life all the way down the slope to the ledge. And then, as we watched, something happened. Susan changed. I wonder what might change someone's mind about whether they wanted to live or die?"
Hudson was silent for a few moments.

Übung 74: Reimen sich die folgenden Wortpaare? Markieren Sie mit richtig ✔ oder falsch –!

ÜBUNG 74 !

1. die, dye ☐
2. her, hair ☐
3. sleep, creep ☐
4. wait, hate ☐
5. look, book ☐
6. good, food ☐
7. sun, moon ☐
8. there, bear ☐
9. thought, that ☐

"You're thinking that someone pushed her, and that drove her to commit suicide? Isn't that a bit far-fetched, Inspector?"
"Not if the person who tried to kill her was her nearest and dearest," said Hudson, thoughtfully. "Perhaps that is what she couldn't face. Captain, you know as well as I that when a woman is murdered, her husband is one of the first people we investigate. Mel Gordon said several things over the last couple of days that suggest he is fighting some kind of inner demon."

"What did he say?"

"Mel had an almost military level of preparedness for this adventure," said Hudson, slowly. "The rest of us were treating the tour as a holiday, whereas Mel seemed to anticipate trouble at every turn. He was on edge, Captain – so to speak."

ÜBUNG 75 !

Übung 75: Verbinden Sie die folgenden Sätze jeweils mit Hilfe der vorgegebenen Konjunktion! Setzen Sie ein Komma, wo nötig!

1. I did it. I thought it was right. (**because**)

___

2. He studied hard. The semester ended. (**until**)

___

3. He acts. He owns the place. (**as if**)

___

4. I will still feel bad. He apologises ((apologizes)). (**even if**)

___

5. She will not go. He goes. (**unless**)

___

6. I stayed home. Bob went. (**so**, im Sinne von **consequently**)

___

7. I stayed home. Bob could go. (**so**, im Sinne von **in order that**)

___

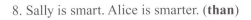

8. Sally is smart. Alice is smarter. (**than**)

____

The Captain stopped tapping his fingers and listened.
"There were times when Mel would tense up about something, and Susan would look at him protectively," said Hudson. "Perhaps it was only after he tried to kill her that Susan realised that Mel was beyond her help. Perhaps she felt this to be a personal failure."
"Most people wouldn't take this a sufficient reason to kill themselves," said the Captain. "After all, it was his problem, not hers."
"If this had been going on for years," said Hudson, "it might have become Susan's problem as well. Think of everything we've learnt about the way a marriage will slowly organise ((organize)) itself around the problems of one of the partners."
Captain Harvey looked down at his hands. "For example, when the husband is an alcoholic?" he asked.
"For example," confirmed Hudson, and sighed.

Übung 76: Setzen Sie die Verben in die richtige Zeitform des Konditional!

Sometimes hikers report UFO sightings in the Grand Canyon. If I saw a UFO land, I (1. run) ________________ right up to the ship! I (2. wave) ________________ to the aliens! If they (3. be) ________________ nice to me, I (4. ask) ________________ them for a ride. If they (5. say) ________________ no, I (6. understand) ________________. If they (7. ask) ________________ me to take them home, I (8. take) ______________ them to my place immediately. They (9. know) ____________ that I am secretly one of them.

"Susan called Mel's name on her way down," Hudson continued.
"The others all remember that," confirmed the Captain. "Marie cried and said that Susan wanted her husband."
"Or she wanted us to get him," suggested Hudson.
The Captain looked at Hudson in surprise.
"Let's put it more neutrally," said Hudson. "Calling Mel's name was ambiguous. Susan may have wanted her husband's help – and also wanted us to help him. In any case, she may well have been pointing us towards our man."
The Captain nodded.
"There's something else that may be affecting how we remember that cry. Every one of us feels terribly responsible for the death of Susan Gordon," said Hudson, evenly. "We stood there and watched her die."

! ÜBUNG 77

Übung 77: Plural-s oder Genitiv-s? Unterstreichen Sie die richtige Form!

1. The problem is her's/hers.
2. Those are the children's/childrens' toys.
3. All the mother's/mothers were invited to tea.
4. The candies/candy's were decorated with chocolate icing.
5. Will you go home for the holidays/holiday's?
6. Many secrets/secret's went with him to the grave.
7. They listened to a story about forty thieves/thief's.
8. The women/women's scarves were black.

"You did everything that could have been done," said Captain Harvey. "Bob Snyder was down there in a matter of minutes."
"But we weren't fast enough to save her." Hudson paused. "Have you ever been close to someone who committed suicide, Captain?"
"No," admitted the Captain.
"The people left behind find it hard to accept. Susan turned her back on us and jumped. Captain, we feel abandoned and betrayed – and very guilty. I believe these feelings may have coloured (*colored*) how we remember –."
Just then there was a knock at the door, and a man in a grey suit let himself in.

Übung 78: Welche Gegensätze gehören zusammen! Ordnen Sie zu!

! ÜBUNG 78

1. love	☐ despair
2. rage	☐ sorrow
3. moodiness	☐ shame
4. joy	☐ confidence
5. hope	☐ calmness
6. pride	☐ hate
7. fear	☐ cheerfulness

"Excuse me," he said. "I'm Agent Wagner of the Federal Bureau of Investigation ((FBI))."
"How do you do," said Inspector Hudson. "I am Inspector James Hudson of Scotland Yard."
The men shook hands.
"You may know that the Park Police and the FBI work together to investigate suspected crimes on federal land. I'll be the FBI investigator on this case. I came as soon as I heard the news."

Inspector Hudson nodded. “I see.”

“We appreciate your cooperation, as we don’t yet know what happened to Susan Gordon.”

Captain Harvey frowned.

“I’m sorry we meet under such trying circumstances, Inspector,” said Agent Wagner. “I understand you were a witness to the death of Susan Gordon in Grand Canyon earlier this morning.”

“Yes, I was,” replied Inspector Hudson.

“I’m really sorry,” said Agent Wagner. “It must have been awful to come to Grand Canyon on *vacation*, thinking you would escape the kind of crime you must deal with regularly over there, and then –.”

The Agent spread his hands.

“It was indeed rather dreadful,” said Inspector Hudson. “I was just explaining to the Captain here how difficult it is for people who are close to a suicide to deal with their feelings of guilt. We all wish we could have done something to prevent Susan’s death.”

“I was reading your initial account of the incident, Inspector,” said Agent Wagner. “I understand you have some reservations about calling this a suicide?”

ÜBUNG 79 !

Übung 79: Infinitiv oder Partizip? Unterstreichen Sie die richtige Form der Verben!

1. I find it difficult to deal/dealing with people like him.
2. Grand Canyon is worth to visit/visiting.
3. We enjoy to play/playing golf.
4. Has she finished to make/making a fuss?
5. Would you mind telling/to tell me what’s going on?
6. I remember to meet/meeting him at a conference.

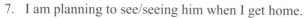

7. I am planning to see/seeing him when I get home.
8. Jack is busy preparing/to prepare the party.
9. I would like to visit/visiting London.
10. I remembered to go/going to her flat for tea.

"I am trained to consider every possibility," said Hudson, carefully. "In detective work, it is extremely important to keep an open mind."
"Maybe you could fill me in on what you've been discussing with Captain Harvey."
Inspector Hudson explained his doubts and suspicions to the FBI Investigator.

Übung 80: Setzen Sie das richtige Possessivadjektiv ein!

ÜBUNG 80 !

1. Gloria and Vinnie love ___________ grandchildren.

2. Sarah has forgotten ___________ car keys.

3. I brought ___________ hairbrush.

4. Did you remember ___________ toothbrush?

5. My sister and I said goodbye to ___________ parents.

6. Put the hammer in ___________ proper place.

7. Loyalty to ___________ country is part of patriotism.

"There's something else troubling me," said Hudson. "It has to do with Susan's change of heart, down there on the ledge."
"It does seem very strange," said Captain Harvey. "Why would someone who was pushed then turn around and jump?"

Inspector Hudson struggled for words. “On our tour, Ranger Bob talked about a strange phenomenon that sometimes leads to a person’s death. The canyon has a mesmerising ((mesmerizing)) effect.”

“Please, Inspector,” said Captain Harvey. “I’m a practical man. My job is to solve mysteries, not make them up. Don’t tell me you think the Grand Canyon is haunted.”

Übung 81: Schreiben Sie die Kurzformen im folgenden Abschnitt aus!

“I don’t 1. ______________ think a ghost told Susan to jump,” Hudson assured the Captain. “That’s 2. ______________ not what I mean. But the vast, inhuman space of the Grand Canyon seems to call to some people. Have you ever heard of the death instinct?”

“I’m 3. ______________ sorry, Inspector. You’ve 4. __________ lost me. I usually deal with criminals whose motives are pretty simple. I’m 5. ______________ more familiar with the will to live,” said Captain Harvey.

“That’s 6. ______________ one instinct,” agreed Hudson. “The life instinct. But if you’ll 7. ______________ excuse my bringing up Sigmund Freud –.”

The Park Police Captain rolled his eyes.

“Freud said that we have a second instinct, namely, the death instinct. It's 8. ________________ an urge to put our personal identity aside, and merge with the universe. I've 9. ____________ just spent several days in Grand Canyon, and I must say, it exerts a powerful draw. One's own life seems so small in comparison. The canyon is so beautiful, and so peaceful, and so … grand."

"There's one problem, Inspector," said Captain Harvey. "If you listen to that siren call, you wind up dead."
"That is indeed the problem," replied Hudson.

*Übung 82: **S** oder **C**? Setzen Sie die richtigen Buchstaben ein!*

ÜBUNG 82 !

1. excu_e 2. suspi_ious 3. uncon_ _iou_ly 4. advi_ing

5. sui_ide 6. con_iderable 7. advan_ing 8. fier_e

9. lo_e 10. espe_ially 11. magnifi_ent

"So you think that maybe it was only once she was down there on the ledge that she, let's say, heard the call?"
"I cannot swear to what she was thinking," said Hudson. "I can only report what I saw."
Hudson sighed, reliving those moments.
"Susan fought to grasp anything that would help break her fall. She was trying to live, not to die. She listened to my instructions to look at the wall of the canyon. I didn't want her to look out over the abyss and panic. She followed my instructions to shift her weight so that she was well balanced. She was doing very well."
"So what happened?"

Übung 83: Setzen Sie das richtige Possessivpronomen ein!

1. That handbag belongs to Jane. It's ____________.

2. I worked hard on the essay. The ideas are all ____________.

3. Please take this. Here, it's ____________!

4. He won the award. It's ____________.

5. Maura and Caitlyn agreed to share the room. It's ____________.

6. My sister and I inherited the house. It's ____________.

"Ranger Bob's descent set off a shower of pebbles. Susan picked her head up at the sound. She knew she would be saved – which also meant going back up to face Mel. The call of the canyon may have tipped the balance. She looked out over the canyon, took a deep breath, steadied herself, and sprang."

Agent Wagner stroked his chin.

"I don't know much about psychology," he said. "*But I hear what you're saying* ((I understand what you mean)). This has given us enough to think about that I feel justified in detaining *Mr.* Gordon, if only for a few more hours. I'll have our detectives search for data on Mr. Gordon. They'll check to see whether he has any prior record of trouble with the law. We'll check whatever we can find: his medical records, financial records, military records, and whatever else we can dig up."

"It's amazing what you can find on the internet these days," said Inspector Hudson.

"It has changed the nature of law enforcement, *that's for sure* ((to be sure))," agreed Agent Wagner. "The rest of you are free to leave the police station. In fact, I've already told Ranger Bob that he could go back to work. However, I would appreciate it if you would all *stick around* ((remain close by)) for another day or so."

Übung 84: Sind die folgenden Ausrufe britisch, amerikanisch oder beides?

1. Wow! ____________________
2. I say! ____________________
3. Bloody well right! ____________________
4. Blimey! ____________________
5. Brilliant! ____________________
6. For sure! ____________________

"I had been planning on it," answered Inspector Hudson. "I suppose we won't get to the waterfall in Havasu Canyon, after what happened. Still, Grand Canyon is so beautiful that I would be happy to spend some time resting up and admiring the view from the veranda of the hotel."

"I can understand that the canyon has taken on a different meaning for you after this morning," apologised ((apologized)) Agent Wagner. "I'm sorry that the experience could not have been more positive."

"I deal with such matters professionally," said Inspector Hudson. "I'm more concerned about the other members of my group."

"'Death in Grand Canyon', wasn't that the title of your tour?" remarked Agent Wagner. He sighed, shrugging his shoulders. "I guess you got your money's worth."

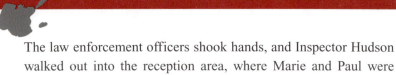

The law enforcement officers shook hands, and Inspector Hudson walked out into the reception area, where Marie and Paul were already waiting. Together, they stepped into the glaring sunlight.

ÜBUNG 85 !

Übung 85: Verbinden Sie die beiden Sätze mit Hilfe eines Partizips!

1. Susan breathed slowly. She held on to the tree.

____

2. The Captain walked in. He shuffled the papers.

____

3. The park ranger hiked off. He whistled a popular tune.

____

4. Marie looked at Inspector Hudson. She bit her lip.

____

5. The Captain looked at Inspector Hudson. He drummed his fingers on the desk.

____

____

6. He waited. He expected an answer.

____

7. The park ranger hesitated. He hoped he was wrong.

____

"This has been the worst morning of my life," lamented Marie.
"It's hard to believe it began with that gorgeous sunrise," Paul said.
"That was quite some hike. Speaking of which, we haven't eaten anything but trail mix in hours. You know what the ranger said about making sure we get enough to eat and drink."
"How can you think about eating at a time like this!" exclaimed Marie.
"He's right, Marie," confirmed Inspector Hudson. "It has been a terrible day, but we must keep up our strength."
"What do you say we have lunch at the café a couple of blocks down?" suggested Paul.
The three hikers sat down to lunch, and even Marie found herself eating more than she would have thought possible. Over coffee and cake, they relaxed a bit. Inspector Hudson noticed that even their posture had changed, as relief and fatigue set in. Marie looked absolutely exhausted.
"It's just so awful," whimpered Marie. "And my poor cousin Mel has had such a hard life."
"Now, now," said Paul. "We needn't go bothering (*don't need to bother*) Inspector Hudson with those old stories."
Hudson noticed that Paul's voice was a bit stern for someone who had just experienced a shocking death in the family.
"Maybe you're over it," sniffled Marie. "But to me, it's still as if it happened yesterday."

Übung 86: Setzen Sie jeweils die richte Form in die Lücke!
(he, my, his, her, him, himself)

ÜBUNG 86 !

She appealed to Inspector Hudson with 1. __________ eyes.

"2. __________ cousin Mel had a hard time of it as a teenager," she recounted. "3. __________ father died when he was only twelve. He seemed unsure of 4. __________ after that. 5. __________ would go out of 6. __________ way to do dangerous things, almost as if 7. __________ were daring death to take 8. __________, too. 9. __________ got into trouble a lot. Mel dropped out of *college* ((university)) in 10. __________ first year and joined the army."

"What did he do in the army?" asked Inspector Hudson.
Marie hesitated, and her husband gave her a dark look.
"He was a paratrooper," she said.
Inspector Hudson nodded and kept a straight face. "And what happened?"
"I'm not sure what happened," said Marie. "Like most of what Mel started, it didn't last. Before long, he was home again. He was *dishonorably* (dishonourably) discharged."
Paul looked away and pursed his lips.
"He was never quite right after that," said Marie. "Before, when he would get into trouble, at least he had a certain sense of … daring, James. A sense of adventure."
Paul put his head in his hands.
"After he came home from the army, he was quieter; you might even say, withdrawn. He always looked as if he hadn't gotten enough sleep."
Marie's face softened.
"When he met Susan, we all hoped for the best. Mel brightened up. They really loved one another, you know. That's why I don't believe he could have pushed her, James. It's just not possible. Susan meant everything to Mel."
Inspector Hudson nodded encouragingly.

Übung 87: Lesen Sie weiter und unterstreichen Sie im folgenden Absatz alle Verben im Present Perfect und im Present Perfect Continuous!

"In the years since they were married," continued Marie, "things have gotten better for Mel. He got a steady job at last, thanks to Paul.

It's not easy, you know, trying to get a job after you've been *dishonorably* discharged. People always wonder what you might have done."

"And you don't know?" probed Hudson.

Paul spoke up. "I don't," he said. "But I know Mel is a good worker. He's quiet, but he's no longer the terror he was when he was younger. Susan did him a world of good."

"They were trying to start a family," added Marie. "They've been trying for a few years. I had the feeling that Susan was getting discouraged. Mel wasn't taking it well.

I think it brought up a lot of insecurities he had about being left behind after his own father's death. He must have been worried about whether he would be a good father – or even whether he would be a father at all."

Inspector Hudson looked discreetly at his watch.

"Well, Susan and Mel both seemed a bit down," said Marie. "That's when Paul and I decided to invite them on a trip to Grand Canyon. We thought the natural beauty of Grand Canyon might cheer them up. The *colors* are so beautiful! It's just like in the pictures we saw!" Marie smiled for a moment.

"We thought that the sheer size of the canyon might somehow help them put their problems in perspective. I'd also heard from so many people that the stress of trying to have a child can really work

against the couple. It often happens that if they go away on *vacation* and forget about it – 'it' happens!"
She smiled again briefly.

ÜBUNG 88 !

Übung 88. Mit Apostroph oder ohne Apostroph? Unterstreichen Sie die richtige Form!

1. It's/Its time to go home.
2. Bob and Jim said their/they're planning to drive to California.
3. I asked Laura if the textbook were mine or hers/her's.
4. Do you know whether its/it's still possible to get tickets?
5. The team lost it's/its standing in the competition.
6. The boat lay on it's/its side.
7. Do you know whether or not theirs/there's an extra water bottle?
8. The mule picked up it's/its ears to listen.
9. I wonder if it's/its going to rain tonight.
10. They should let me know if there's/theirs anything I can do to help.

"Paul and I knew that money was tight for Susan and Mel. Mel's job doesn't pay all that much, and they were saving for the baby. So Paul and I thought we would offer to pay for this *vacation*."
"Marie," said Inspector Hudson, softly. "You didn't tell all of this to the police, did you?"
"No," she said. "What does it have to do with what happened today?"
"We don't know yet," said Hudson, "but we need to find out – for Mel's sake, as well as for Susan's. Please excuse me. I need *to make a phone call* (to ring up s.o.)."

Übung 89: Setzen Sie die Sätze ins Aktiv!

1. Mel's holiday was paid for by Marie.

2. The prize was won by the lady in the blue dress.

3. The grammar exercises were done correctly by the students.

4. John is being helped by Ramon.

5. The work has been finished by me.

6. The documents have been received by Daniel.

7. The homework will have been completed by Philip on Monday.

8. The new museum director will be hired by Sarah.

9. The painting will be signed by the artist.

10. Two sculptures are going to be cast by the foundry.

____

"Excuse me," Inspector Hudson said to the waiter. "Is there a public phone, please?"
"We no longer have one, sir."
"It's terribly urgent," said Inspector Hudson. I must contact the police."
"You are welcome to use my *cellphone* (mobile)," he replied. He punched in the number and handed the phone to Inspector Hudson.
"May I speak to Agent Wagner immediately, please? This is Inspector Hudson, with urgent news."
Inspector Hudson quickly reported what he had learnt from Marie about Mel's past.

ÜBUNG 90 !

Übung 90: Auf was kann ein Fallschirmspringer nicht verzichten? Lösen Sie das Kreuzworträtsel!

1. The opposite of despair

_ _ ☐ _

2. The branch of the military service that operates on the ground

☐ _ _ _

3. How one might feel when things are not going well

_ _ _ _ _ _ ☐ _ _ _ _

4. The first four years of university in America

☐ _ _ _ _ _ _

5. To release from military service

_ _ _ _ ☐ _ _ _ _ _

6. The opposite of secure

_ _ _ _ _ ☐ _ _

7. An exciting and possibly dangerous undertaking

_ _ _ _ _ ☐ _ _ _

8. A person between 13 and 20 years of age

_ _ ☐ _ _ _ _ _

Lösung: _ _ _ _ _ _ _ _

"We must let the detectives who are searching Mel Gordon's flat know that they should look for any evidence they can find concerning Mel Gordon's military service. Marie just told me that Mel was dishonourably (*dishonorably*) discharged from the army. She doesn't know the details, but he seems to have been traumatised ((traumatized)) by his experience in the paratroops."
"The paratroops?"
"The chaps ((guys)) who jump out of planes," confirmed Inspector Hudson.
"I read you, Hudson. I'll call the detectives right away."
"The detectives are still at his *apartment*," said Agent Wagner hurriedly. "The bad news is that Captain Harvey released Mel Gordon almost an hour ago."
"Oh, no!" exclaimed Inspector Hudson.
"Captain Harvey believed we had no grounds to keep Gordon," said Agent Wagner. "But let's not waste time discussing that. I will come by in my car immediately to pick you up."
Inspector Hudson rushed back to the table. "Come on," he cried. "We are leaving immediately to look for Mel Gordon!"
Inspector Hudson threw several five-dollar *bills* (banknotes) at the waiter, and they ran out to the street.

ÜBUNG 91

Übung 91: Ist der Satz richtig übersetzt? Markieren Sie mit richtig ✔ oder falsch –!

1. ☐ Du sollst die Tür immer fest schließen./You are supposed to always close the door tightly.
2. ☐ Man soll die Wahrheit sagen./One should tell the truth.
3. ☐ Das Wetter soll morgen wirklich schön sein./The weather is supposed to be very nice tomorrow.
4. ☐ Er sagte, er sollte um achtzehn Uhr zurück sein./He said he should be back at six o'clock.
5. ☐ Das Theaterstück soll schlecht geschrieben sein./The play should be badly written.
6. ☐ Sie soll nach Ägypten gegangen sein./She should have gone to Egypt.

Agent Wagner's car screeched to a halt.
"Get in!" he cried.
"I know where he is," said Marie.
"He's not at the hotel," said Agent Wagner. "I already called."
"He is back at the first place we stood and looked out over Grand Canyon."
Agent Wagner looked at Marie in the rear view mirror.
"How do you know?" he asked.
"Remember back on the first day, at the very first overlook? 'Buena Vista', I think it was called. Ranger Bob was telling us about people who went over the edge," she said, looking to the others. "I came up to Mel as he was gazing out over Grand Canyon. He didn't look good."
They waited for her to continue.
"Mel said to me, 'This is as good a place as any to die'."

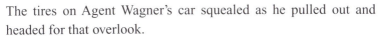

The tires on Agent Wagner's car squealed as he pulled out and headed for that overlook.
"Buckle up," he ordered. "This is going to be a fast trip."
Agent Wagner turned on his siren and leant on the horn. Tourists scattered in all directions as the police car took off.

Übung 92: Unterstreichen Sie das richtige Modalverb!

1. I can't/won't read your mind.
2. Dennis shouldn't/wouldn't smoke so much.
3. I should have/could have mailed that letter, because I said I would.
4. I must have/could have forgotten my keys, because they're not in my pocket.
5. You needn't have/shouldn't have brought such a lovely gift!
6. You needn't have/shouldn't have lied to the police officer!
7. You can't have/needn't have thought that was a good idea!

Agent Wagner tossed his *cellphone* to Inspector Hudson.
"Hit redial," he ordered. "Ask those detectives what they've found so far."
Inspector Hudson did as he was told.
"Good evening," he said. "This is Inspector Hudson of Scotland Yard."
"Well, hello, sir. Agent Wagner told us about you. He said you were from Scotland Yard."
"Indeed, I am," replied Inspector Hudson. "He and I are just now on the road that leads to Buena Vista, overlooking Grand Canyon."
"Getting in a bit of sightseeing, sir?"

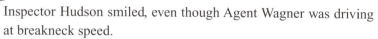

Inspector Hudson smiled, even though Agent Wagner was driving at breakneck speed.
"Sir?" asked the detective. "Are you alright? I thought I heard a police siren in the background."
"Quite right ((That's right))," said Inspector Hudson. "We are in a bit of a hurry to get to Buena Vista."

! ÜBUNG 93

Übung 93: Wie lauten die britischen Entsprechungen der folgenden Wörter/Wendungen?

1. *period* ________________
2. *canned* ________________
3. *ornery* ________________
4. *go to the bathroom* ________________
5. *zero* ________________
6. *styrofoam* ________________
7. *creek* ________________

"When he sent us to search *Mr.* Gordon's *apartment*, Agent Wagner told us that you suspected something was up with Mel Gordon," said the detective. "Our detectives had already started running a data check on him, and they found the *dishonorable* (dishonourable) discharge right away. But once you called Agent Wagner to tell him what you had *learned* (learnt) from Marie Johnson, we had a better idea what to look for."
"Tell me, have you turned up anything?"
"We found letters dating from the time of Gordon's discharge from

the army, sir. There were also letters to his future wife. You already know that Gordon had volunteered for the paratroops, and gone through jump school. On his first time out, he refused to jump.
The letters are somewhat incoherent, sir. It's not clear from his own accounts in these letters whether he fell or was thrown out of the plane. What is clear is that he was severely traumatized (traumatised) by the experience."
"How can you tell, detective?"
"Sir, he describes the event over and over and over. The details change a little every time, but it's as if he can't help repeating the experience."

Übung 94: Geben Sie die amerikanischen Entsprechungen der folgenden Wörter an!

ÜBUNG 94 !

1. biro ______________________
2. flat ______________________
3. mobile ______________________
4. torch ______________________
5. knapsack ______________________
6. banknote ______________________
7. holiday ______________________

Agent Wagner's car screeched to a halt in the parking lot. Wagner and Hudson ran full tilt to the overlook. Mel Gordon was already standing at the guard rail, gazing into Grand Canyon.

Startled, Mel looked up. He *leapt* (leaped) up onto the low stone wall.

"Don't come any closer or I'll jump!" he cried.

Wagner and Hudson halted.

"It's alright, Mel," said Agent Wagner.

"How can you possibly say it's alright?" snarled Mel. "My wife is dead, and I killed her!"

"Easy, Mel," said Wagner.

"Nothing is alright in my life," said Mel. "Nothing at all."

"Do you want to tell us about it?" asked Inspector Hudson.

Mel hesitated.

"My father would kill me," he said. "I'm such a failure."

"What do you mean?" asked Inspector Hudson, in his calm voice, moving a little bit closer to Mel.

"I wanted to show him that I could do it," said Mel. "That I was brave. That I had grown up alright, and that he could be proud of me."

"Mel, I want to tell you something very important," said Inspector Hudson. "It's not your fault that your father died."

Mel looked at his feet and faltered.

ÜBUNG 95 !

Übung 95: Vervollständigen Sie die folgenden Sätze mit den entsprechenden Question Tags!

1. He's in a lot of trouble, ____________________?
2. Shemsy did well on the exam, ____________________?
3. You're going to London, ____________________?
4. They were planning to visit us, ____________________?

5. Reuben did say he was coming, ________________?

6. Carlos wasn't gone long, ________________?

7. They didn't forget to water the plants, ________________?

8. I'm not next, ________________?

9. You'll be back soon, ________________?

10. She think she's sure to win, ________________?

11. You won't forget this lesson, ________________?

"I was always in trouble," said Mel, looking up at Inspector Hudson. "I was bad in school, and I dropped out of college. I joined the army, thinking I could do that right."

"I understand you signed up for the paratroops," said Inspector Hudson.

"What was I thinking?" asked Mel. "You tell me! I was the kid who was afraid of the seesaw!"

Inspector Hudson nodded. "What happened, Mel?"

"Jump school was bad enough," said Mel. "I watched guys lay down their gear and walk away. And it was just like the officers promised: no one said a word. Why didn't I just walk away?"

Inspector Hudson nodded.

Übung 96: Setzen Sie das richtige Fragewort ein! Die folgenden Wörter können auch mehrfach verwendet werden.
(when, why, what, how)

ÜBUNG 96 !

1. __________ does "death instinct" mean?

2. __________ did Inspector Hudson find the answer?

3. __________ is the sky blue?

4. Joseph wasn't sure exactly __________ it happened, but it was shortly after sunset.

5. Do you know __________ to pilot a plane?

6. __________ if he had stayed in college?

7. __________ does the park ranger get down to the ledge?

8. I don't understand __________ anyone does what they do.

9. Bob wanted to be a park ranger __________ he grew up.

"The day came for the first jump," said Mel. "I had checked my chute a dozen times. I knew the drill. But when the jump master gave the order, 'Stand up and hook up!' –."
Mel raised his hands helplessly.
"Nothing happened."
"Nothing happened?"
"I couldn't do it. I couldn't even stand up. Two guys on either side of me picked me up off the floor and hooked me up to the line."
Mel's face was blank.
"I don't know what happened," he said.
"Did you jump?"

ÜBUNG 97 !

Übung 97: Sind die folgenden grammatischen Konstruktionen britisch, amerikanisch oder beides?

1. The company are planning a new product line. __________

2. The company is bankrupt. __________

3. Alan ordered the shrimps. ______________________________

4. Did she write a poem yesterday? ______________________________

5. Did you clean your room yet? ______________________________

6. Have you cleaned your room yet? ______________________________

7. The Colorado River was muddy. ______________________________

8. The army crossed the River Thames. ______________________________

9. They should have got the tickets today. ______________________________

10. They should have gotten the tickets today. ______________________________

"Once you're hooked up, you can't exactly not jump," said Mel. "That overhead line leads right to the door of the plane. Everybody slides down the line, and out you go. I got dumped."

"Dumped?"

"The next thing I knew, I was out there in the middle of nowhere. My jump school reflexes took over, and there I was, flying through the clear blue sky."

"Just like Susan," said Paul. He and Marie had walked up quietly as Inspector Hudson was talking with Mel. "Except that Susan didn't have a parachute."

"I don't know what happened!" shouted Mel. "I didn't mean to kill her! Susan meant everything to me!"

"It's alright, Mel," said Inspector Hudson, soothingly. "Just step down here and we can talk."

Agent Wagner took Paul and Marie aside.

"Please stay back," said Agent Wagner, softly. "Please stay back."

ÜBUNG 98 !

Übung 98: Geben Sie jeweils die britische und die amerikanische Form des Simple Past der folgenden Verben an!

	britisch	amerikanisch
1. leap	__________	__________
2. loan	__________	__________
3. lean	__________	__________
4. dream	__________	__________
5. spell	__________	__________
6. kneel	__________	__________
7. smell	__________	__________
8. spill	__________	__________
9. learn	__________	__________
10. mean	__________	__________

The officers of the Park Police and the park rangers who had responded to the emergency call quietly urged everyone back. They kept a respectful distance so that Inspector Hudson could talk to Mel.

"Susan was the only person who understood!" cried Mel. "Every night, when I would wake up with nightmares about falling out of the plane, Susan would tell me it was alright. I would be fine, she said."

"You're not fine!" shouted Paul. "You're a psychopath and a killer! You're not a man!"

A Park Police officer grabbed Paul and hauled him behind a tree. "Susan said I was fine!" screamed Mel. He turned towards the canyon and looked to the horizon. "Susan loved me! Susan –."

"Oh, no!" screamed Marie.

Mel screamed all the way down.

"Susan!"

Übung 99: In welchen Sätzen wird das Futur richtig verwendet? Kreuzen Sie an!

ÜBUNG 99 !

1. a) ☐ Once she is the headmistress, she will not tolerate rude behaviour (*behavior*).
   b) ☐ Once she is the headmistress, we will not behave badly.
   c) ☐ Both.

2. a) ☐ I shall be there at eight o'clock.
   b) ☐ I shall be waiting at eight o'clock.
   c) ☐ Both.

3. a) ☐ We will waiting for you at the restaurant.
   b) ☐ We wait for you at the restaurant.
   c) ☐ We will be waiting for you at the restaurant.

4. a) ☐ The train leaves tomorrow morning at nine.
   b) ☐ The train is leaving tomorrow morning at nine.
   c) ☐ Both.

5. a) ☐ In June, they will marry for twenty-five years.
   b) ☐ In June, they will have been married for twenty-five years.
   c) ☐ In June, they are being married for twenty-five years.

6. a) ☐ I going to meeting Rachel for dinner.
   b) ☐ I'm meeting Rachel for dinner.
   c) ☐ I'm having met Rachel for dinner.

"Please stand back, everyone," said Agent Wagner. He gestured to the uniformed officers to push back the small knot of people who had gathered.
Agent Wagner and Inspector Hudson walked over to the low stone wall. They already knew what they would see when they leant over the guard rail.
"Blue sky and Grand Canyon," said Inspector Hudson. "As Ranger Bob would say."
"I'm really sorry," said Agent Wagner. "You might have talked him down, Hudson."

ÜBUNG 100

Übung 100: Setzen Sie die Verben in die richtigen Zeitformen!

In the distance, a raven (1. hover) ________________ on the canyon winds.

"But I (2. do not) ________________, (3. do) ________________ I?"

Agent Wagner's gaze (4. sink) ________________.

"That (5. be) ________________ the second time today." Inspector Hudson, too, (6. look) ________________ down.

"I (7. fail) ________________ two people."

"It (8. be) ____________________________ not your fault," (9. say) ________________ Agent Wagner. "You (10. be) ________________ a good man, Hudson. Now (11. let) ________________'s get out of here. Captain Harvey's people (12. know) ________________ what (13. do) ________________."

Agent Wagner and Inspector Hudson walked slowly back to the car. "You understand that we'll have to record your account of this incident, as well?" asked Agent Wagner.
"You mean Mel Gordon's death?"
Wagner nodded.
"I don't mind," said Inspector Hudson. "It's Mel's cousin Marie I'm worried about."

Übung 101: Will-Future oder Future Perfect? Setzen Sie die Verben in die richtigen Formen des Futurs!

ÜBUNG 101 !

In just a few lines, you will reach the end of *Death in Grand Canyon* and arrive at the final exam. Inspector Hudson (1. solve) ________________________ another case! In reading the novel, you (2. complete) ________________________ over ninety exercises. Then, you (3. write) ________________________ the final exam. Do you think you (4. do) ________________________ well on the test? I wonder whether you (5. enjoy) ________________________ the book. I hope we (6. meet) ________________________ again for another adventure!

"Didn't you say that once already today?"

Inspector Hudson shook his head. "This is getting a bit disorienting."

"Stay away from that canyon rim," cautioned Agent Wagner.

"I believe I've heard that before, too," said Hudson. "That, and 'drink lots of water!'."

Agent Wagner smiled. "I'm afraid we sound like a broken record – and now you know why. But seriously, what are you going to do after this?"

Inspector Hudson looked out the window at the alien landscape.

"I'd like to go home," he admitted. "I promised both my housekeeper and my superior in London that I would rest up and stay out of trouble. I must confess, I've had about enough of 'Death in Grand Canyon'."

Agent Wagner and Inspector Hudson laughed, and pulled in to the police station.

Abschlusstest

Übung 1. Simple Present oder Present Continuous? Setzen Sie die Verben in die richtige Form!

"I (1. go) ________________ to the library," said Ayesha. "Are you (2. come) ________________ ?"

"Must you always (3. go) ________________ to the library?" exclaimed Kathleen. "(4. do not) ________________ you ever (5. have) ________________ any fun?"

"Of course I (6. have) ________________ fun!" said Ayesha. "But this week, I (7. study) ________________ for the final exam in maths (*math*). It is supposed to be very difficult, and Dr Smith (8. say) ________________ we (9. have, study) ________________ hard if we (10. want) ________________ to do well."

"I (11. guess) ________________ you are right," grumbled Kathleen. "But I (12. want) ________________ to go to the party."

"I (13. plan) ________________ to leave the library at eight-thirty," said Ayesha. "Now you (14. talk) ________________. Let's (15. go) ________________!"

Übung 2: Setzen Sie die unregelmäßigen Verben ins Simple Past!

1. have ____________________
2. do ____________________
3. drive ____________________
4. teach ____________________
5. put ____________________
6. get ____________________
7. run ____________________
8. keep ____________________

Übung 3: Bilden Sie die verneinte Form der folgenden Sätze! Notieren Sie die vollständige Verneinung sowie die Kurzform!

1. Kamal will arrive on time.
   a) vollständige Verneinung: ____________________
   b) Kurzform: ____________________
2. Frank should feel guilty.
   a) vollständige Verneinung: ____________________
   b) Kurzform: ____________________
3. Amisha could get a job in another city.
   a) vollständige Verneinung: ____________________
   b) Kurzform: ____________________

4. Carmelo feels up to the job.

a) vollständige Verneinung: ______________________________

b) Kurzform: ______________________________

5. Angela thought it was too far to walk.

a) vollständige Verneinung: ______________________________

b) Kurzform: ______________________________

Übung 4: Setzen Sie die richtigen Präpositionen ein!

Arlene was 1. ______ her way 2. ______ work when she ran 3. ______ her friend Rachel.

"Arlene! What have you been 4. ______ to?" Rachel cried. "I've looked 5. ______ you 6. ______ every meeting 7. ______ the Wildlife Club!"

"I've been feeling a bit 8. ______ the weather," said Arlene. "But I think I'm 9. ______ it now."

Übung 5: Geben Sie die (eher) amerikanische Schreibweise der folgenden Wörter an!

1. armoured ______________________

2. travelled ______________________

3. modelling ____________________

4. sour ____________________

5. metre ____________________

6. vogue ____________________

7. colonise ____________________

8. harmonise ____________________

9. prize ____________________

10. moisturiser ____________________

11. centre ____________________

Übung 6: Setzen Sie die Verben in die richtige Form und Zeit! Verwenden Sie ein Hilfsverb, wo nötig!

If I (1. travel) ____________________ anywhere in the world, I (2. choose) ____________________ to go to Grand Canyon. I (3. choose) ____________________ a different place, but I have always wanted to see the great empty spaces of the American West. I (4. imagine) ____________________ that you would choose Hawaii, because you like the ocean. There (5. be) ____________________ very little water in Grand Canyon, except for the Colorado River! One (6. drink) ____________________ a lot of water in the desert!

Übung 7: Setzen Sie die folgenden Sätze in die indirekte Rede!

1. “I’m going to take my dog for a walk,” said Julia.

2. “Are you sure that’s a good idea, Julia?” asked Anna.

3. “Why wouldn’t it be a good idea?” wondered Julia.

4. “Dogs are sometimes afraid of heights,” observed Anna.

5. “I will take Fido for a walk along the wall,” decided Julia.

6. She explained, “That way, he will not be able to see the canyon!”

7. “That’s a good idea!” exclaimed Anna.

8. She patted Fido and said, “You will like the park!”

Übung 8: Verknüpfen Sie jeweils die beiden Sätze mit Hilfe der vorgegebenen Wörter!

1. Stanley is leaving for France. We won't see him for a while. (**so**)

____

____

2. There was a strike. The construction was delayed. (**as a result**)

____

3. Dr Raymond was not elected. He seemed to be highly qualified. (**though**)

____

____

4. Gregory lives in Arizona. He arrived in 1995. (**since**)

____

5. We have finished our work. I will leave. (**since**)

____

Übung 9: Ergänzen Sie die Sätze mit den passenden Question Tags!

1. Bill's awfully cheerful, __________________?

2. Richard will help us, __________________?

3. Sean really should pay more attention, __________________?

4. Maria tries hard, ________________?

5. They were at the police station, ________________?

6. Shut that door, ________________?

7. I don't see how we could improve, ________________?

Übung 10: Setzen Sie das richtige Possessivpronomen ein!

1. Bob has a book. It's __________.

2. Laura and I own property together. It's __________.

3. Joseph and George run a business. It's __________.

4. I forgot my pen. Did you forget __________, too?

5. I thought I had put __________ in my pocket.

6. Jeanne says the dress is __________.

Übung 11: Mit Apostroph oder ohne Apostroph? Setzen Sie das richtige Wort ein!

1. __________ going to be a long winter.

2. Do you find that Grand Canyon lives up to ________ reputation?

3. The water bottle has Mary's name on it, so I'm sure it is ________.

4. I'm sure ________ a reason for his absence.

5. ________ time we were on our way.

6. The tent belongs to them. It's ________.

7. London has lost ______________ charm, since Mona left for New York.

8. ________ a storm cloud on the horizon.

9. ________ common knowledge that he is leaving.

10. Jack and Ben said they'd come to the meeting, but I don't know whether ________ sister will be in town that day.

11. I thought the book was mine, but Lisa says ____________ ________.

Übung 12: Beantworten Sie die folgenden Fragen zum Text in der richtigen Form des Past Tense!

1. For which law enforcement agency did Agent Wagner work?

____

2. Where did they find Mel in the end?

____

3. What was he doing there?

____

4. What was Mel's job in the army?

____

5. Why did Mel leave the army?

____

6. What did the detectives find in Mel's flat?

____

7. Did Mel and Susan pay for the trip to Grand Canyon?

____

8. What were Inspector Hudson and Agent Wagner doing on their way back to Grand Canyon?

____

Übung 13: Geben Sie die amerikanischen Entsprechungen für folgende Wörter an!

1. windcheater ________________
2. trainers ________________
3. rucksack ________________
4. torch ________________
5. idiot ________________
6. sunrise ________________
7. sweets ________________
8. reception ________________
9. full stop ________________

10. dustbin ____________________

11. flat ____________________

12. stream ____________________

13. polystyrene ____________________

14. mobile ____________________

Übung 14: Welches Wort ist das „schwarze Schaf" in der Reihe? Unterstreichen Sie!

1. pullover, trousers, trainers, torch, shirt
2. *oatmeal*, bacon, eggs, tomato, pancake
3. parachute, marriage, army, discharge, Mel
4. violet, blue, silver, yellow, asbestos
5. Navajo, Puerto Rican, Pueblo, Hopi, Havasupai
6. *cellphone, vacation,* trainers, *backpack, apartment*
7. travelling, signalling, rappelling, *modeling*
8. Buena Vista, Grand Canyon, Flying Convertible Point, London

Lösungen

Übung 1: 1. exclaimed 2. sat 3. continued 4. handed 5. looked 6. gasped 7. meant 8. ordered

Übung 2: 1. a 2. a 3. an 4. a 5. a 6. an 7. some 8. an 9. some

Übung 3: 1. small 2. Mars 3. supervisor 4. nonsense 5. interest 6. brochure

Übung 4: 1. *colorful* 2. *honor* 3. hour 4. *savor* 5. *labor* 6. *flavor* 7. our 8. *favorite* 9. glamorous 10. your

Übung 5: 1. a 2. a 3. b 4. a 5. a 6. b

Übung 6: 1. Inspector Hudson is a detective at Scotland Yard. 2. He lives in London. 3. Inspector Hudson's first name is James. 4. No, he is British. 5. No, he does not usually wear colourful clothing. 6. Yes, he owns hiking boots. 7. Yes, Inspector Hudson is hungry. 8. The Grand Canyon is in Arizona. 9. Yes, he feels a bit out of place.

Übung 7: 1. amerikanisch 2. britisch 3. beides 4. beides 5. beides 6. beides 7. britisch 8. amerikanisch 9. beides

Übung 8: 1. began 2. thought 3. took 4. had 5. was 6. left 7. bought 8. went

Übung 9: 1. vest – *undershirt* 2. trousers – *pants* 3. windcheater – *windbreaker* 4. pullover – *sweater* 5. pants – *underpants* 6. trainers – *sneakers*

Übung 10: 1. Whose hat is this? 2. How often does he wear it? 3. How much did it cost? 4. How did he guess the answer? 5. Where did he fly? 6. Why was Mel so short with Bob? 7. What did the rangers recommend? 8. When did Inspector Hudson arrive? 9. How many pullovers did she have? 10. Where can I purchase the hat?

Übung 11: 1. 16 2. 2 3. 4 4. 12 5. 3 6. 36 7. 16

Übung 12: 1. tours 2. robberies 3. murders 4. visits 5. holidays 6. states 7. people 8. lives

Übung 13: 6, 4, 1, 3, 5, 2

Übung 14: 1. pavement 2. designed 3. murder 4. hat 5. trail 6. ranger 7. clothing Lösung: vertigo

Übung 15: 1. began 2. jumped 3. started 4. scolded 5. pretended 6. turned 7. continued 8. notified 9. ran

Übung 16: 1. embarrassed – proud 2. polite – rude 3. early – late 4. finishing – beginning 5. magical – rational 6. dawn – dusk 7. stylish – unfashionable 8. working – playing

Übung 17: 1. regularly 2. genuinely 3. heartily 4. clearly 5. shortly 6. pleasantly 7. broadly

Übung 18: 1. choose 2. stepped 3. get 4. dropped 5. groaned 6. seems 7. wanted 8. look 9. called 10. turn 11. take 12. lifted 13. went

Übung 19: 1. flat – Wohnung 2. adventure – Abenteuer 3. raft – Floß 4. awaken – aufwachen 5. incredible – unglaublich 6. body – Körper 7. ledge – Felsvorsprung 8. parachute – Fallschirm 9. lunge – sich stürzen 10. dare – sich wagen

Übung 20: 1. of 2. on 3. of 4. to 5. for 6. into 7. of

Übung 21: In 5. ist **to** eine Präposition. In allen anderen Fällen ist **to** Teil eines Verbs im Infinitiv.

Übung 22: 1. her 2. your 3. his 4. his 5. our 6. our

Übung 23: 1. to get 2. get 3. gets 4. gets 5. gets 6. got 7. get 8. got

Übung 24: 1. *colorful* 2. crimson 3. orange 4. yellow 5. Gold 6. Gold 7. copper 8. silver 9. violet 10. blue 11. azure 12. turquoise

Übung 25: 1. Western territory was acquired by the United States. 2. The land was mapped by surveyors. 3. Louisiana was sold by France. 4. The canyon was lit up by the sun. 5. The story was told by Ranger Bob. 6. The Colorado River was named by Francisco Tomás Garcés. 7. The Colorado River was explored by Powell.

Übung 26: 1. You are not afraid. 2. You aren't afraid. 3. The are not thirsty. 4. They aren't thirsty. 5. You were not right. 6. You weren't right. 7. She is not going. 8. She isn't going. 9. I am not going. 10. I'm not going.

Übung 27: 1. night 2. light 3. might 4. flight 5. eight 6. freight 7. flight 8. thought

Übung 28: 1. Powell 2. settled 3. explore 4. disaster 5. ferocious 6. underway 7. smashed 8. equipment 9. dwindling 10. quit 11. unable

Übung 29: 1. Nobody 2. nothing 3. Anybody 4. Nothing 5. anywhere 6. Everybody 7. Everywhere 8. anything

Übung 30: 1. ... he knew nothing about it. 2. ... on doing it her way. 3. ... the truth of the story. 4. ... that it didn't seem likely. 5. ... but he wasn't sure. 6. ... to say what might have happened.

Übung 31: 1. He claimed that they murdered/had murdered an Indian woman. 2. Sumner testified that he had given them his watch for safekeeping. 3. His sister confirmed that the watch was very valuable. 4. His men grumbled that he was a terrible leader. 5. Dunn said that Powell tried/had tried to kill him. 6. After the attack on Dunn, the men said that they no longer trusted Powell. 7. Powell asked Sumner why he should believe him. 8. Many Westerners say that they still believe that Powell was a hero.

Übung 32: 1. who 2. whose 3. whom 4. that 5. who 6. which 7. that 8. who

Übung 33: 1. richtig 2. falsch 3. falsch 4. richtig 5. falsch 6. richtig 7. richtig 8. falsch 9. richtig 10. richtig

Übung 34: 1. Paiute 2. Navajo 3. Havasupai 4. Pueblo 5. Hopi 6. Havasupai

Übung 35: 1. …into the eighties. 2. …fifteen degrees. 3. … below freezing. 4. … seventy on the coast. 5. … up to six miles per hour. 6. … from the south. 7. … sunny and mild. 8. … cloudy and cold.

Übung 36: 1. It's 10:15. 2. It's 7:30. 3. It's 7:50. 4. It's 6:15. 5. It's 5:45. 6. It's 11:40.

Übung 37: 1. Lie 2. lied 3. lies 4. lays/laid 5. lies 6. to lie 7. lay 8. lay 9. lay 10. lain 11. lied 12. was laying

Übung 38: 1. and 2. and 3. or 4. so 5. and 6. but 7. or 8. so 9. or, or

Übung 39: 1. sprang 2. serious 3. film 4. copycat 5. insured 6. difficult 7. altogether Lösung: suicide

Übung 40: 1. newer, newest 2. faster, fastest 3. smaller, smallest 4. bigger, biggest 5. worse, worst 6. funnier, funniest 7. simpler, simplest 8. prettier, prettiest

Übung 41: 1. travelling 2. signalling 3. modelling 4. programme 5. jewellery 6. judgement 7. arguement 8. ageing

Übung 42: 1. He cut his finger. 2. The corpse is often cut into pieces. 3. Are you an experienced typist? 4. No, I was hiking. 5. She misjudged the difficulty of the trail. 6. "Does he have this problem, too?"

Übung 43: 1. They're 2. their 3. there 4. There 5. Their 6. they're 7. they're 8. their

Übung 44: 1. as dead as a doornail 2. as dry as a bone 3. as cold as ice 4. as light as a feather 5. as quick as a fox 6. as clear as mud

Übung 45: 1. much 2. a lot 3. a little 4. many 5. Few 6. Most 7. Few 8. a few

Übung 46: 1. was writing 2. was singing 3. were hiking 4. was putting away, rang 5. was doing, got 6. was playing, called 7. were sure, scored

Übung 47: 1. a 2. b 3. b 4. a 5. b 6. b 7. b 8. a

Übung 48: 1. mule 2. billion 3. ton 4. half-pint 5. continent 6. journey

Übung 49: 1. good 2. well 3. good 4. well 5. well 6. well 7. good 8. good 9. well 10. good 11. well

Übung 50: 1. come 2. stay 3. are 4. travel 5. risk 6. trouble

Übung 51: 1. confirmed 2. rescue 3. effective 4. hiker 5. temperature 6. shivering 7. injured 8. helicopter

Übung 52: 1. a 2. a 3. c 4. a 5. a 6. a

Übung 53: 1. b 2. a 3. b 4. a 5. b 6. a

Übung 54: 1. A US billion is ten to the ninth power. 2. That means that a US billion has nine zeroes. 3. A British billion has twelve zeroes. 4. A US billion is a thousand million. 5. A British billion is a million million. 6. A US trillion is equal to a British billion. 7. In fact, most Britons today use the US standard. 8. Inspector Hudson is one of the few people who care.

Übung 55: 1. get 2. getting 3. get 4. got 5. getting 6. getting 7. get 8. got

Übung 56: 1. *styrofoam* 2. panorama 3. promontory 4. emergencies 5. measles 6. dehydration 7. intravenous

Übung 57: 1. … he gasped 2. … she wondered 3. … he asked 4. … they shouted 5. … she asserted 6. … he said

Übung 58: 1. vorwiegend britisch 2. amerikanisch 3. beides 4. vorwiegend britisch, amerikanisch veraltet 5. britisch 6. vorwiegend amerikanisch, aber auch zunehmend im Britischen verwendet 7. amerikanisch 8. beides

Übung 59: 1. rolled 2. was 3. was (not) 4. went 5. turned 6. grabbed 7. broke 8. screamed

Übung 60: 1. Breathing 2. laughing 3. lying 4. hanging 5. adapted 6. Hanging 7. Thinking 8. balancing

Übung 61: 1. realize 2. organize 3. surprise 4. *dialog* 5. *analog* 6. *catalog* 7. *check*

Übung 62: 1. "This voice was very different." 2. "That English person – what was his name again?" 3. "That strange accent," she thought. 4. "What is he doing here?" 5. "What am I doing here?" 6. "She was over the edge of the Grand Canyon." 7. "For someone who is about to –," she thought. 8. "His voice was beautiful." 9. "She had always wanted to go to London." 10. "Maybe everything would be fine." 11. "She would *take a vacation.*" 12. "She would go to London." 13. "But the words came out wrong." 14. "Everything was wrong."

Übung 63: 1. Put 2. wait 3. Eat 4. Tell 5. Don't move 6. don't wait 7. Don't think 8. Don't try

Übung 64: 1. … in the dark 2. … what you're doing! 3. … for her 4. … you later! 5. … for a long time. 6. … television.

Übung 65: 1. am going 2. go 3. are going 4. is going 5. is thinking 6. thinks 7. say 8. try (im Sinne von ‚prinzipiell')/are trying (im Sinne von ‚in dieser speziellen Situation')

Übung 66: 1. two 2. too 3. into 4. to 5. to 6. too 7. to 8. into

Übung 67: 1. Mel Gordon looked strangely calm. 2. "Please don't blame yourselves," said Bob. 3. Inspector Hudson looked at each member of the group. 4. He remembered Susan crying out. 5. He remembered Bob's bravery. 6. He rappelled down the crumbling rock to get her. 7. What on earth had happened? 8. Why did she jump? 9. "We all saw it," said Paul. 10. "We saw her jump."

Übung 68: 1. Ranger Bob called them because Susan went over the edge. 2. Because it was an emergency, the rangers came on the double. 3. Although it had happened years ago, she still remembered. 4. Even though he was short on money, he insisted on paying. 5. Marie is safe above, whereas Susan is in big trouble. 6. I jumped because she dared me to do it.

Übung 69: 1. to 2. to 3. towards 4. to 5. towards 6. towards 7. to

Übung 70: 1. Can 2. Could 3. May 4. Can 5. might 6. may 7. could 8. would

Übung 71: 1. … if he tried. 2. … play the piano. 3. … to lift very heavy boxes. 4. … already read when I was four. 5. … touch your toes? 6. … tell me the time, please?

Übung 72: 1. flower 2. break 3. bear 4. close 5. weigh 6. reign 7. Which/witch/which

Übung 73: 1. cheerfully 2. sadly 3. competently 4. agreeably 5. surprisingly 6. suspiciously Lösung: rangers

Übung 74: 1. richtig 2. falsch 3. richtig 4. richtig 5. richtig 6. falsch 7. falsch 8. richtig 9. falsch

Übung 75: 1. I did it because I thought it was right. 2. He studied hard until the semester ended./Until the semester ended, he studied hard. 3. He acts as if he owns the place. 4. I will still feel bad, even if he apologises./Even if he apologises, I will still feel bad. 5. She will not go unless he goes./Unless he goes, she will not go. 6. I stayed home, so Bob went. 7. I stayed home so Bob could go. 8. Sally is smarter than Alice.

Übung 76: 1. would run 2. would wave 3. were 4. would ask 5. said 6. would understand 7. asked 8. would take 9. would know

Übung 77: 1. hers 2. children's 3. mothers 4. candies 5. holidays 6. secrets 7. thieves 8. women's

Übung 78: 1. love – hate 2. rage – calmness 3. moodiness – cheerfulness 4. joy – sorrow 5. hope – despair 6. pride – shame 7. fear – confidence

Übung 79: 1. to deal 2. visiting 3. playing 4. making 5. telling 6. meeting 7. to see 8. preparing 9. to visit 10. to go/going

Übung 80: 1. their 2. her 3. my 4. your 5. our 6. its 7. one's

Übung 81: 1. do not 2. That is 3. I am 4. You have 5. I am 6. That is 7. you will 8. It is 9. I have

Übung 82: 1. excuse 2. suspicious 3. unconsciously 4. advising 5. suicide 6. considerable 7. advancing 8. fierce 9. lose 10. especially 11. magnificent

Übung 83: 1. hers. 2. mine. 3. yours 4. his. 5. theirs. 6. ours.

Übung 84: 1. beides 2. britisch 3. britisch 4. britisch 5. britisch 6. amerikanisch

Übung 85: 1. Susan breathed slowly, holding on to the tree. 2. The Captain walked in, shuffling the papers. 3. The park ranger hiked off, whistling a popular tune. 4. Marie looked at Inspector Hudson, biting her lip. 5. The Captain looked at Inspector Hudson, drumming his fingers on the desk. 6. He waited, expecting an answer. 7. The park ranger hesitated, hoping he was wrong.

Übung 86: 1. her 2. My 3. His 4. himself 5. He 6. his 7. he 8. him 9. He 10. his

Übung 87: 1. (things) have gotten better 2. (you')ve been *dishonorably* discharged 3. (you might) have done 4. (They've) been trying 5. (He must) have been worried

Übung 88: 1. It's 2. they're 3. hers 4. it's 5. its 6. its 7. there's 8. its. 9. it's 10. there's

Übung 89: 1. Marie paid for Mel's holiday. 2. The lady in the blue dress won the prize. 3. The students did the grammar exercises correctly. 4. Ramon is helping John. 5. I have finished the work. 6. Daniel has received the documents. 7. Philip will have completed the homework on Monday. 8. Sarah will hire the new museum director. 9. The artist will sign the painting. 10. The foundry is going to cast two sculptures.

Übung 90: 1. hope 2. army 3. discouraged 4. military 5. college 6. discharge 7. insecure 8. adventure 9. teenager Lösung: parachute

Übung 91: 1. falsch 2. richtig 3. richtig 4. richtig 5. falsch 6. falsch

Übung 92: 1. can't 2. shouldn't 3. should have 4. must have 5. needn't have 6. shouldn't have 7. can't have

Übung 93: 1. full stop 2. tinned 3. nasty 4. use the toilet 5. nought 6. polystyrene 7. stream

Übung 94: 1. *ballpoint pen* 2. *apartment* 3. *cellphone* 4. *flashlight* 5. *backpack* 6. *bill* 7. *vacation*

Übung 95: 1. isn't he 2. didn't she 3. aren't you 4. weren't they 5. didn't he 6. was he 7. did they 8. am I 9. won't you 10. doesn't she 11. will you

Übung 96: 1. What 2. How 3. Why 4. when 5. how 6. What 7. How 8. why 9. when

Übung 97: 1. britisch 2. amerikanisch 3. britisch 4. beides 5. amerikanisch 6. beides 7. amerikanisch 8. britisch 9. britisch 10. amerikanisch

Übung 98: 1. leapt, *leaped* 2. leant, *loaned* 3. leant, *leaned* 4. dreamt, *dreamed* 5. spelt, *spelled* 6. knelt, *kneeled* 7. smelt, *smelled* 8. spilt, *spilled* 9. learnt, *learned* 10. meant, *meant*

Übung 99: 1. c 2. c 3. c 4. c 5. b 6. b

Übung 100: 1. hovered 2. didn't 3. do 4. sank 5. was 6. looked 7. failed 8. is 9. said 10. are 11. let 12. know 13. to do

Übung 101: 1. will have solved 2. will have completed 3. will write 4. will do 5. will have enjoyed 6. will meet

Lösungen Abschlusstest

Übung 1: 1. am going 2. coming 3. go 4. Don't 5. have 6. have 7. am studying 8. says 9. have to study 10. want 11. guess 12. want 13. plan 14. are talking 15. go

Übung 2: 1. had 2. did 3. drove 4. taught 5. put 6. got 7. ran 8. kept

Übung 3: 1. a. Kamal will not arrive on time. b. Kamal won't arrive on time. 2. a. Frank should not feel guilty. b. Frank shouldn't feel guilty.

3. a. Amisha could not get a job in another city. b. Amisha couldn't get a job in another city. 4. a. Carmelo does not feel up to the job. b. Carmelo doesn't feel up to the job. 5. a. Angela did not think it was too far to walk. b. Angela didn't think it was too far to walk.

Übung 4: 1. on 2. to 3. into 4. up 5. for 6. at 7. of 8. under 9. over

Übung 5: 1. *armored* 2. *traveled* 3. *modeling* 4. sour 5. *meter* 6. vogue 7. colonize 8. harmonize 9. prize 10. *moisturizer* 11. *center*

Übung 6: 1. could travel 2. would choose 3. might have chosen 4. could imagine/would imagine 5. is 6. must drink

Übung 7: 1. Julia said that she was going to take her dog for a walk. 2. Anna asked if Julia were sure that was a good idea. 3. Julia wondered why it wouldn't be a good idea. 4. Anna observed that dogs are sometimes afraid of heights. 5. Julia decided that she would take Fido for a walk along the wall. 6. She explained that that way Fido would not be able to see the canyon. 7. Anna exclaimed that that was a good idea. 8. She patted Fido and said that he would like the park.

Übung 8: 1. Stanley is leaving for France, so we won't see him for a while. 2. As a result of the strike, the construction was delayed./The construction was delayed as a result of the strike. 3. Dr Raymond was not elected, though he seemed highly qualified./Though Dr Raymond seemed highly qualified, he was not elected. 4. Gregory has lived in Arizona since 1995./Since 1995, Gregory has lived in Arizona. 5. Since we have finished our work, I will leave./I will leave, since we have finished our work.

Übung 9: 1. isn't he 2. won't he 3. shouldn't he 4. doesn't she 5. weren't they 6. would you 7. do you

Übung 10: 1. his 2. ours. 3. theirs 4. yours 5. mine 6. hers.

Übung 11: 1. It's 2. its 3. hers 4. there's 5. It's 6. theirs 7. its 8. There's 9. It's 10. their 11. it's, hers

Übung 12: 1. Agent Wagner worked for the FBI. 2. In the end they found Mel at the first lookout point called 'Buena Vista'. 3. Mel was standing at the guard rail and gazing into Grand Canyon. 4. Mel was a paratrooper in the army. 5. Mel left the army because he was dishonourably discharged. 6. The detectives found letters in Mel's flat. 7. No, they didn't. Paul and Marie payed for the trip 8. On their way back to Grand Canyon, Inspector Hudson *made a phone call* while Agent Wagner was driving the car.

Übung 13: 1. *windbreaker* 2. *sneakers* 3. *backpack* 4. *flashlight* 5. *jerk* 6. *sunup* 7. *candy* 8. *lobby* 9. *period* 10. *garbage can* 11. *apartment* 12. *creek* 13. *styrofoam* 14. *cellphone*

Übung 14: 1. torch 2. tomato 3. marriage 4. asbestos 5. Puerto Rican 6. trainers 7. *modeling* 8. London